*The Well-Tempered
Clavier by
Johann Sebastian Bach*

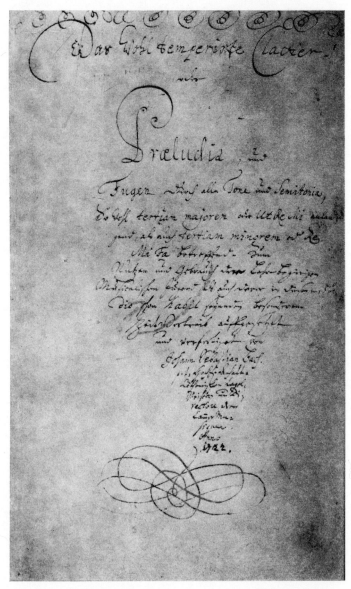

Reduced facsimile of the original, in the possession of the Deutsche Staatsbibliotek, Berlin. (*Signatur BB Mus. ms Bach P 415*)

The Well-Tempered Clavier by Johann Sebastian Bach

HERMANN KELLER

Translated by Leigh Gerdine

W · W · Norton & Company · Inc · New York

First American Edition 1976

This translation © George Allen & Unwin (Publishers) Ltd 1976

Originally published in German under the title
Das Wohltemperierte Klavier
© Bärenreiter-Verlag Kassel, 1965

ISBN–0–393–2187–4

Printed in Great Britain
in 11 pt Baskerville type
by Butler & Tanner Ltd, Frome and London

TRANSLATOR'S PREFACE

The work of Hermann Keller, who was killed in an auto accident in August of 1968, has an uncommon interest for me. When I first discovered his book, *Phrasierung und Artikulation*, I was planning to write such a book myself, although from another perspective; finding his superior treatment of the subject, I was content to translate his work. Largely, I think, as a result of my interest, Carl Parrish then translated his book on the thoroughbass, Walter Buszin the one on improvisation, and Helen Hewitt that on the organ works. Unfortunately Dr Buszin's book has not been published, although the others have appeared.

Keller was a practical musician; his scholarship was thorough and direct. He applied his study to areas of major importance: this I find significant, for I am keenly conscious that the PhD scholarship of American universities tends to produce studies which fill in the gaps of knowledge. The incipient scholar (for whom the PhD thesis may be the first and final piece of "scholarship") all too often will select for study the works of a composer too obscure yet to have been exhumed. His subsequent teaching risks an over-emphasis on minutiae. Presumably before such scholarship rests, all the gaps will have been filled in. That has its importance.

Keller dealt with issues in the main stream of music: if the resultant book be brief – as *Phrasing and Articulation* is – so much the better. Most of the books I read could be condensed into a fraction of their pages. One mourns the trees sacrificed needlessly. In passing, it is astonishing that Keller's *Phrasing and Articulation* is, in 1976, the only book to deal with a subject of such great significance to music.

In this book Keller treats *The Well-Tempered Clavier* analytically as well as musically. His suggestions for the performer are based upon the best contemporary scholarship, focused in practical terms. At the time of his writing of this book, the New Bach *Ausgabe* had not yet published the volume containing *The Well-Tempered Clavier*. To date, that volume, to be edited by Walter Gerstenberg, still has not appeared. Its eventual appearance may well raise new, additional questions.

In his own preface to this book, Keller mentions "the large

number of general meritorious 'companions' to *The Well-Tempered Clavier,*" a first "introduction to the work" ... which "originate almost without exception in foreign countries" ... among them England and the United States. It ought to be embarrassing to our national pride, given the scholarly emphasis of our graduate schools and the easy availability of recordings, that the general standard of Bach performance should, in 1976, be so little advanced; that every new book in English on *The Well-Tempered Clavier* must deal afresh with the elementary. Perhaps this book will advance that standard.

Keller mentions the work of Werker, Czackes and David in particular: the reader who wishes more detail will want to consult them. I have taken the liberty of correcting measure numbers where Keller – or his typographer – has obviously erred. In a few rare cases, I have been rash enough to register some disagreement with Keller: the reader will find these disagreements generally relegated to footnotes, which he may prefer to discount.

Three German words, *Kontrapunkt, Durchführung* and *Praller,* have given special problems in translation:

Kontrapunkt: This, of course, translates as "counterpoint." However, wherever a fugue has a regular countersubject to which Keller refers simply as the *"Kontrapunkt,"* I have carefully substituted the term "countersubject." In fugal analysis it seems to me helpful to designate the countersubject as such. Cases in point would include the reference, page 54, to the "countersubject of the C Minor Fugue, Book I," or the reference to the countersubject of the G sharp Minor Fugue in Book II, page 183.

Durchführung: This word is more troublesome, and there is no easy solution. I have not translated it as "development," preferring in my own brand of pedantry to reserve "development" to the Classic forms, particularly the middle section of a movement in sonata form. Where (rarely) that technique is involved, as in the D Major Prelude in Book II, I have indeed used the word "development." Generally, I have translated *Durchführung* as "Exposition," occasionally as "Re-exposition." I have tried to use the word "Exposition" to mean any organized set of *dux/comes* or *comes/dux* entries. A case in point would be the C Sharp Major Fugue in Book I, page 58, where there are several references to an "incomplete exposition," which might have been called, in someone else's vocabulary, an "incomplete development." In the instance of the E Flat Minor Fugue in Book I, I have used "Exposition," because when there are so many re-expositions, the value of distinguishing them so specifically only from the original exposition seems doubtful. With this conception of the Exposition and Re-exposition, then, the "Episodes" become those linking sections where the subject is aggressively absent.

Praller: This term is especially important, and I have translated it as *pralltrill* in order to avoid calling the ornament an "inverted mordent." As I have explained in a footnote at an appropriate place, the *pralltrill* differs from the inverted mordent by appearing *on* the beat, rather than *before* it, as the Romantic composers used it. So much is this habit ingrained in keyboard players that even to call the ornament an "inverted mordent" is to invite a Romantic interpretation of it. Using the term *pralltrill*, then, would seem to me to require a slightly greater effort, and to have a hope of achieving the Baroque intent:

    1] that the trill begin on the beat;

    2] that, with few exceptions, the trill begin with the upper neighbor in whatever the key is at the moment, not with the principal note; and

    3] that there should be several alternations of the notes in the trill.

If a personal note is not inappropriate, I much prefer the sound of the more dissonant note on the beat, and where (if rarely) there is a choice, I customarily opt for the more dissonant interpretation, the strong presence of the non-harmonic tone. In some such choices there is latitude for disagreement.

Measure numbers in this volume refer to measure numbers in the *Urtextausgabe* published in the Peters Edition as No. 4691A (Book I, edited by Alfred Kreutz) and No. 4691B Book II, edited by Hermann Keller). The importance of reading this book with the music at hand cannot be over-emphasized – preferably the editions cited.

The reader will note that Keller set out initially to deal with only Book I of *The Well-Tempered Clavier*, and later added a complete consideration of Book II as well: for this reason, I have had to clarify rather frequently in the early part of the book the fact that Keller is making reference at that point only to works in Book I. I have also retained a few foreign words as being of general usage: *galant* and *empfindsam*, for example, as references to special styles of the period coming on at the end of Bach's lifetime.

Differences between English and American usage of musical vocabulary are by now familiar; nevertheless, because this translation is to appear simultaneously in England and in the United States, an apology should be made to British readers. I inhabit an American academic institution, consequently I have used the American vocabulary throughout: the text refers to "half notes" rather than to "minims," to "quarter notes" rather than to "crotchets," and the like. American spelling has been used as well. For British readers, I sincerely hope that Keller's substance will atone for what must seem a lack of elegance.

Brief mention – totally inadequate to their contributions – of several people who have helped this translation appear is imperative: first, Geraint Jones, whose interest re-opened the possibility of publication after I had given the project up, who improved the flow of language to such a degree as almost to have re-translated the book (but who is blameless for what inadequacies remain); Dr Paul Pisk, friend, colleague, scholar's scholar, great musical spirit and teacher of us all, who has checked that the German has been accurately translated; Kendall Stallings, who has checked details, including such tedia as measure numbers just one more time; Isobel Gants, my super-competent secretary, who saw the copy through multiple versions with care; Roberta Gardner, who gave me some emergency typing of the manuscript; Rayner Unwin, whose personal intervention prevented the project from being forgotten; and finally Claire Brook of W. W. Norton, who brought a rare and scholarly grasp of the subject to the final editing of the manuscript.

Webster College, St Louis, Missouri   Leigh Gerdine
August 1, 1976

CONTENTS

"... It was there for the first time, with complete peace of mind and without outside distraction, that I gained a conception of your Grand Master. I expressed it thus: it was as though eternal harmony conversed with itself, as it might have come to pass in the bosom of God, shortly before the creation of the world. So moved was I by it in my inmost consciousness that it seemed to me I neither possessed nor needed ears, least of all eyes, nor any other senses."

A letter from Goethe to Zelter on June 21, 1827, when the organist von Berka had played to him from *The Well-Tempered Clavier*.

"The preludes and fugues of The Well-Tempered Clavier *are the Old Testament, the sonatas of Beethoven the New Testament, of the pianist."*

Hans von Bülow

FOREWORD

The Well-Tempered Clavier of Johann Sebastian Bach, this "work of all works," as Schumann called it, has generated a great number of commentaries. The present book is intended, above all, to help in performance; it will combine what the layman wants to know about it with what the professional ought to know. Beyond that, it will provide the player, especially one who uses an *Urtext* edition, with advice on the performance of the preludes and fugues. In so doing, this book takes a position midway between the two groups into which one might divide the monographs on *The Well-Tempered Clavier*. On the one side stands a large number of general, meritorious "companions" to *The Well-Tempered Clavier* which give a first introduction to the work. These originate almost without exception in foreign countries, among them England, France, Holland, Italy, Belgium and the USA. In Germany, on the other hand, theorists (including in the last decade or so, Wilhelm Werker, Ludwig Czackes and Johann Nepomuk David) have written learned works, particularly about the fugues and their relationship with the preludes. Czackes mentions the preludes not at all; David sees in them only "a place for the preparation of the fugue subject." This treatment does not do *The Well-Tempered Clavier* justice. The preludes not only merit equal consideration with the fugues – but many of them are of greater individual significance than their fugues; it is therefore misguided to regard *The Well-Tempered Clavier* as a theoretical work, perhaps as a "manual on the composition of fugues" (Riemann). Many newer analyses with preconceived schoolboy concepts of fugue go still further, dissecting the movements into the tiniest details, but asking nothing whatever about their musical significance. Others seek to uncover the secret structure of the fugues. But through this kind of approach Bach's work is deflected ever farther from its true intention. Bach did not seek to present an esoteric, learned work to his composing contemporaries, but, as his title expresses clearly and precisely, he "wrote down his composition for the use of musical young people eager to learn, as well as to provide a special pastime for those already proficient in this study." *The Well-Tempered Clavier* is clearly meant to be played by young people as well as by musically cultivated amateurs; to the latter, Bach, with an almost touching modesty, promises a "special pastime." One should be found with *The Well-Tempered Clavier* not at the writing desk, but rather at an instrument, "playing." And as in Bach's time practice and theory were not yet separated as they are today, the player derived from the book not only an introduction to all the twenty-four keys, but also to the texture and form of the preludes and fugues. This unity has been lost to us, but one can find it again in *The Well-Tempered Clavier*. And more than that: the player can experience again what Goethe expressed in his famous letter to Zelter, which we placed at the beginning of this work as a motto. Whoever today plays the preludes and fugues of *The Well-Tempered Clavier* from an *Urtext* edition, in which he encounters Bach without the intervention of an editor, will be confronted with a series of questions which he cannot immediately answer. To that player this book will be a guide. It speaks in the first instance of what is common to all the preludes and fugues of *The Well-Tempered Clavier* in order later to allow the special character of each individual prelude or each individual fugue to be shown all the more clearly. The author will be no more than a steward, who shows a visitor to a great building with many rooms the overall plan, the function of the individual parts, and any special features. Every individual, once he has found the right entrance, can then penetrate deeper into those regions beyond the range of words.

I dealt with the first part of *The Well-Tempered Clavier* in pages 124 to 158, and the second part in pages 219 to 249, in my book *Die Klavierwerke Bachs* which appeared in 1950 in the Peters edition (Leipzig). I take this opportunity to thank the publishers of that edition for permission to incorporate from that book some portions which are now completely rewritten in the light of the literature which has since appeared and of my own researches.

Hermann Keller

Stuttgart, Spring 1965

INTRODUCTION

Transmittal of the Title

The title, pictured facing title page, in Bach's own gracefully ornate fair copy reads: *Das Wohl temperirte Clavier. oder Praeludia, und Fugen durch alle Tone und Semitonia, so wohl tertiam majorem oder Ut Re Mi anlangend, als auch tertiam minorem oder Re Mi Fa betreffend zum Nutzen und Gebrauch der Lehrbegierigen Musicalischen Jugend, als auch dere in diesem studio schon habil seyenden besonderen Zeitvertreib aufgesetzet und verfertiget von Johann Sebastian Bach. p.[ro] t.[empore] Hochf.[ürstlich] Anhalt-Cöthenischen Capel-Meistern und Directore derer Cammer-Musiquen. Anno 1722.*

("*The Well-Tempered Clavier.* or Preludes and Fugues in all tones and semitones, both with the major third or Ut Re Mi, and the minor third or Re Mi Fa, composed and written down for the profit and use of musical young people eager to learn, as well as for a special pastime for those who are already proficient in this study, by Johann Sebastian Bach, at the present time Capelmeister to the Prince of Anhalt-Cöthen and Director of his Chamber Music. Anno 1722.")

This is the only copy of *The Well-Tempered Clavier* which we possess in Bach's own handwriting Book I only]. This rare manuscript has been in the possession of the former State Library in Berlin for more than a hundred years. Bearing the handwritten date 1732, it represents a fair copy completed ten years after its composition from a lost original manuscript. The year 1722 as the date of either the beginning or end of the work is shown by the watermark of the paper, the similarity of the handwriting with that of the Inventions and Sinfonias (BWV 772 to 801) and the close relationship with the *Klavierbüchlein für Wilhelm Friedemann Bach*, completed in 1720. Two further manuscripts, earlier taken as autograph copies, have been established as copies from the hand of Anna Magdalena and Wilhelm Friedemann Bach. In addition to these, the copies by

Altnikol (the son-in-law of Bach) and Kirnberger (who was a student of Bach from 1739 to 1741) must count as important sources, for Bach used them in teaching and made corrections in them, although he failed to add these changes into his own copy. Of later manuscripts, that of the Hamburg organist Schwencke may be mentioned. A complete listing of the sources will be included in the *Kritischer Bericht*.

One may ask why Bach did not publish this work, which had in his own lifetime achieved a certain recognition within the broader circle of his friends and students. Apparently he was afraid, at a time when the *empfindsam* and *galant* style counted for everything, that the market would be too limited. Bach's first printed opus, the Six Partitas for harpsichord (BWV 825 to 830), were described by him on the title page as *Galanterien* (which they certainly are not), to make them palatable to the fashionable public. Nevertheless, in the half century after his death, the fame of *The Well-Tempered Clavier* was already so great that at the beginning of the nineteenth century, in the years 1800 to 1802, no fewer than three publishers printed *The Well-Tempered Clavier*: Hoffmeister and Kühnel in Leipzig, Simrock in Bonn, and Nägeli in Zürich. Since then almost countless editions of *The Well-Tempered Clavier* have appeared, of which a critical review will be given in pages 202 to 204.

Genesis

At the end of 1717, "after an obstinately forced resignation," Bach had gone from Weimar with a dishonorable discharge to the court of the young, music-loving Prince Leopold of Anhalt-Cöthen. He had been employed at Weimar for ten years as a violinist (since 1714 as concertmaster) and organist of the Court Chapel. In Cöthen he was numbered no longer in the rank of the liveried valets of the Prince, but had the title of *Hofkapell-meister* and "director of Chamber Music." He had neither school nor church services to look after, for the court was Reformed; he took his place among the higher court officials and had time and leisure to compose. Like every musician of the Baroque, he composed such music as his duties demanded; in Cöthen therefore above all he wrote chamber music and clavier works. After long, almost over-long years of learning, he was now at the age of thirty-five at the height of his first mastery. Where the Duke of Weimar had seen in him only a useful subject, his new provincial prince knew what a rare bird he had captured in his little province. Everything combined to make the few Cöthen years among Bach's happiest and most fruitful: the recognition which he found, the leisure for his own creations, and indeed his recent conjugal bliss with Anna Magdalena Wülckens, a young chamber singer at the court, whom he carried over the threshold in 1721 after the death of his first wife, Maria Barbara. Thus the wealth and the significance of the works for clavier and chamber music created in Cöthen are almost unimaginably great. The chamber music includes the Brandenburg Concertos (BWV 1046 to 1051), the violin concertos, the sonatas for violin (also for flute, gamba) with obbligato harpsichord (BWV 1014 to 1019), the sonatas and partitas for unaccompanied violin (BWV 1001 to 1006) and many others. Among the compositions for the clavier (clavichord or harpsichord), we find the little preludes and fugues, the English and French suites (BWV 806 to 817), the Chromatic Fantasy (BWV 903), the Inventions and Sinfonias (BWV 722 to 801) and *The Well-Tempered Clavier*, Book I (BWV 846 to 869). Six little preludes, the Inventions and Sinfonias as well as eleven preludes from *The Well-Tempered Clavier* are found in their earlier shape in the *Klavierbüchlein für Wilhelm Friedemann Bach*, to which the father put the finishing touches on the 22nd of January 1720 for his beloved, then nine-year-old son.[1] It appeared in 1962 incorporating the most recent researches edited by Wolfgang Plath in the new *Bach-Ausgabe* V/5 [BA 5021], with *Kritischer Bericht* 1963. At the same time, Bach was working on the fifteen two- and three-part Inventions and Sinfonias, which were completed in 1723. That Bach found the time in addition to "prepare" a still greater collection of works in so short a period astonished his students. Ernst Ludwig Gerber, a son of Bach's student Heinrich Nikolaus Gerber, wrote in his *Historisch-biographisches Lexikon der Tonkünstler* (Historic-biographic Dictionary of Composers), which appeared in 1791, that Bach may have composed the Inventions and Sinfonias "in a short time when he was without an instru-

---

[1] I edited the *Klavierbüchlein* in 1927 for the first time with Bärenreiter-Verlag as publisher (BA 140). HK.

ment, to dispel ill-humor and boredom." This could have been on one of the journeys on which Bach had to accompany the Prince with other musicians of his Chapel, although this conjecture cannot be proved. We must conclude that, with the exception of three pieces: the Prelude in E Flat Major, the Fugue in D Sharp Minor and the Fugue in A Minor, all of the pieces contained in Book I of *The Well-Tempered Clavier* were either sketched or completed between 1721 and 1722.

Just and Tempered Tuning

What does the remarkable title *The Well-Tempered Clavier* mean? To understand it correctly, it is necessary to clarify the concepts which form the basis of our entire music, about which however professional musicians often know as little as do musical amateurs.

"Just" intervals are those whose frequencies stand in a simple numerical relationship to one another. The frequencies of a fundamental and its octave are related in the ratio 1:2; this closest possible numerical relationship creates the greatest possible consonance. The numerical relationship 2:3 creates the perfect fifth, 3:4 the perfect fourth, 4:5 the "just" major third, 5:6 the "just" minor third. Prime numbers larger than 5 are not used in Western music (consequently the ratios 6:7, 7:8, 10:11, 12:13, etc., are not found). These relationships are shown in the following table, in which the harmonies (upper partial tones whose frequencies consist of multiples of the fundamental) from 1 to 16 are indicated:

1 : 2 : 3 : 4 : 5 : 6 : 8 : 9 : 10 : 12 : 15 : 16

The first six partial tones create the major triad as a natural consonance. As elements of melodic structure, 8:9 and 9:10 provide the wholetone, 15:16 the halftone. In "just" major, the diatonic notes within an octave correspond to the relationships $1:\frac{9}{8}:\frac{5}{4}:\frac{4}{3}:\frac{3}{2}:\frac{5}{3}:\frac{15}{8}:2$. But these tonal relationships are usable only in monophonic diatonic chant and *a capella* polyphonic singing under certain conditions (perhaps in the style of Palestrina) ; should music wish to reach farther, e.g., modulate to more distant keys, it comes into conflict with disturbing irregularities. For example, in the table above, the wholetone C to D is larger than the D to E; a third C to E constructed from four fifths on top of one another (c to g to d′ to a′ to e″) is larger than a "just" third; twelve fifths on top of one another are more than seven octaves; and so on. It therefore becomes necessary to even out these differences, to make them regular, to "temper." After several intermediate stages, a compromise solution was found at the end of the seventeenth century which is still used today, viz. to divide the octave into twelve equal parts. This is the so-called *equal temperament*, in which all intervals, with the exception of the octave, are a little "impure," but are all equidistant from each other in every key. Now for the first time one could use all keys, and modulate from one to any of the others. Certainly the loss of purity was unfortunate, but incomparably greater was the gain which music drew from it. The man to whom the discovery of this innovation is ascribed (which had already been demanded in the sixteenth century by far-seeing men) was the organist and organ-builder Andreas Werckmeister, who in 1691 published a work which bore the following title: *Musicalische Temperatur/ oder deutlicher und wahrer mathematischer Unterricht/wie man ... ein Clavier, sonderlich die Orgelwerke, Positive, Regale, Spinetten und dergl. wohltemperiert stimmen könne* ... "Musical Temperament/or clear and correct mathematical instruction/how to tune a clavier, particularly organs, positives, regals, spinets, and the like in equal temperament." Werckmeister's book thus dealt only with instruments of fixed pitch, i.e., keyboard instruments (claviers), and only from them the new technique was gradually transferred to melody instruments. Composers took possession of the newly discovered territory, which had been shown to them, at first hesitantly, then with ever-increasing boldness. Pachelbel used seventeen keys in his suites, J. K. F. Fisher in his *Ariadne musica*, a collection of preludes and little fugues for organ, used nineteen major and minor keys and the Phrygian mode on E. The first to use all twenty-four keys was not Bach, but Mattheson, who in 1719 wrote figured-bass exercises in all the keys in his *Die Exemplarische Organistenprobe* (Exemplary Test Pieces for

Organists). (Examples from it are in my *Thoroughbass Method*, tr. and ed. Carl Parrish, W. W. Norton, 1965.) But the incomparably greater achievement of being the first to write music in all twenty-four keys rightly belongs to Bach. However, even Bach did not use all the keys except in *The Well-Tempered Clavier*. The tonalities C Sharp Major, D Flat Major, D Sharp Minor, F Sharp Major, A Flat Major, G Sharp Minor, B Flat, are not found anywhere else in his music, E Flat Minor and B Major only in the trios of dance movements. Karl Philipp Emanuel Bach, the most audacious harmonist of his time, made use of some of these keys; several, such as G Sharp Minor and D Sharp Minor, are rarely encountered even today.

The Character of the Keys in 'The Well-Tempered Clavier'

Does each key have a character of its own? This question is frequently discussed by amateurs and professionals, for the most part with more vehemence than with expert information. The idea has found as many enthusiastic supporters as opponents.

Since the introduction of equal temperament there is no inherent difference between one key and another, because all semitones are the same size. Absolute pitch, the frequency of the standard A, also plays no role, for in the last 200 years it has been changed several times without affecting our understanding of the character of individual keys. The difference exists only in our imagination: music is not what we hear, but our interpretation of what we hear. Thus, our interpretation of key is determined by the nature and number of the accidentals and by the distance of the key from C as a center. If the sense of music is fixed through melody, harmony, rhythm and meter, and its expression through tempo, dynamics, tone color and articulation, there must still be added to these expressive factors the tonality which the composer chooses. He does this on the basis of tradition and the criteria just mentioned; the music with which he grows up associates itself in his imagination with the character of the key in which it is written. Thus one might trace through a long series of antecedents the character of the Dorian mode which has become our key of D Minor; or of D Major as the tonality in which stringed instruments display the greatest brilliance; or of G Minor as the

tonality in which the Baroque loved to express pomp and
ceremony; for the pastoral G Major is the preferred tonality in
the south, F Major in the north. All these are indications for
the character of certain keys, but in no case attributes fixed for
all time. Often a single work in a specific key is sufficient to
suggest to us possible characteristic attributes: for example,
Bach's Mass (BWV 232) for B Minor, the Fifth Symphony of
Beethoven for C Minor, the so-called "Moonlight" Sonata for
C Sharp Minor, etc. It would be pleasant indeed if one could
say that Bach had been the first to write in all twenty-four keys
and thereby had imprinted these tonalities with a trademark
for all time. That he, like every great composer, had specific
associations with the keys in which he wrote is self-evident, but
that does not make Bach's feeling for a key into a common
denominator. The question of what relationship a prelude and
a fugue have with the tonality in which they lie must be further
dealt with in the individual discussions of each piece of *The
Well-Tempered Clavier* which follow.

The Instrument

If Bach called his selection of preludes and fugues *The Well-
Tempered Clavier*, he understood by "Clavier," a keyboard
instrument, or more precisely, a keyboard instrument with
strings. Andreas Werckmeister, on page 16 of the work cited
above, understood by "Clavier" all keyboard instruments
"particularly organs, the positives, regals" and only then the
"spinets" (harpsichords). Similarly Bach, when he directed "à
2 Clav. e Ped.," left open the question whether the organ or
the pedal harpsichord is intended. By the end of his Weimar
years, however, Bach had completed his stylistic separation of
the organ from stringed keyboard instruments: this is evident
from a comparison of the *Orgelbüchlein* with the clavier works
composed at Cöthen. This raises the question of whether *The
Well-Tempered Clavier* was written for the harpsichord or the
clavichord. Insofar as the compass can give an answer, the
range of the clavichord (C to c''') is nowhere exceeded,[1] while
Bach in the suites *"pour le Clavecin"* perhaps written at the same

---

[1] Keller is here obviously speaking of Book I only of *The Well-Tempered
Clavier*. – Tr.

time, sometimes writes lower than C and (if indeed rarely) goes above d''' at the upper limit. The opinion that *The Well-Tempered Clavier* was written for the clavichord was advanced especially by Forkel, who could rely upon accounts by Wilhem Friedemann and Carl Philipp Emanuel. In his work, *Über J. S. Bachs Leben, Kunst und Kunstwerke* (On J. S. Bach's Life, Art, and Works), published in 1802, he wrote: "The so-called *Flügel* (harpsichords), although capable of great variety, were for him too soulless and the pianoforte was in his lifetime still too much in its infancy, and indeed much too unrefined to be able to satisfy him. He regarded the clavichord as the best instrument for study as well as for domestic private music making [that is, for performance without listeners]. For the expression of his most subtle ideas he found it the most congenial, and he did not believe that such a wide gradation of sound could be created on any kind of *Flügel* (harpsichord) or the pianoforte as on this instrument, poor indeed in sonority but nonetheless extraordinarily flexible." Forkel here repeats the opinion of his time: one must not forget, despite this, that Bach wrote the second movement of the Italian Concerto (BWV 971) for this reputedly "soulless" harpsichord. The Italian Concerto, the French Overture (BWV 831) and the Goldberg Variations (BWV 988) were written "*vor ein Clavizymbel mit zweyen Manualen*" (for a harpsichord with two manuals), but in the first book of *The Well-Tempered Clavier* there is no place where two manuals are required, also nowhere is a change of registration essential within a prelude or a fugue, so that the question of the harpsichord or the clavichord must remain undecided. As Arnold Schering put it (*Aufführungspraxis alter Musik* – Performance Practice of Old Music) in Bach's time such a question would not have been raised. The clavichord with its weak sound was an ideal practice instrument and could serve for "musical entertainments," but in large rooms and public performances performers obviously preferred the harpsichord without troubling themselves about the basic differences between the two instruments. Just as moot is the often-raised question, which pieces in *The Well-Tempered Clavier* are more apt for the clavichord, which for the harpsichord? Argument is pointless because neither of the two instruments exhausts the content of the composition. There is music which can truly be brought to life only on the instrument for which the composer intended it: music of the French clavecinists sounds good only on the "*clavecin*," many pieces of Karl Philipp Emanuel Bach only on the clavichord, the piano sonatas of Beethoven only on the pianoforte. Several fugues of *The Well-Tempered Clavier* would display their full beauty only in an arrangement for chamber music or orchestra (Mozart arranged several for string trio or string quartet [KV 404a and 405]), but the special charm of *The Well-Tempered Clavier* exists precisely in the fact that a mere keyboard instrument, whether it be now the clavichord, the harpsichord, or the pianoforte, must serve as the medium for a music whose content is to be sought beyond the sound. Thus considered, the problem of the present-day piano is basically no different from that of the two instruments of Bach's time. Who can really be satisfied with the performance of the C Major Prelude on the piano, the D Major Fugue on the clavichord, the E Flat Minor Fugue on the harpsichord? The unrealized residue which always remains, however, excites our fantasy so powerfully that we experience *The Well-Tempered Clavier* always again anew, because no interpretation can satisfy us completely or permanently.

Stylistic Elements of 'The Well-Tempered Clavier'

Before the individual stylistic elements of *The Well-Tempered Clavier* are briefly discussed, an introductory attempt must be made to summarize the overall style of the work. Generally Bach is regarded as a typical Baroque musician, his music as the crown and completion of the German Baroque: "Everything leads to him, nothing proceeds from him" (Schweitzer). This is however only conditionally true, and it is especially less true with respect to *The Well-Tempered Clavier* than perhaps to his church music and organ music. Bach, too, was influenced by the great change which took place in music between 1730 and 1770. In his book, *The Commonwealth of Arts*, which appeared in New York in 1949, Curt Sachs described this change as the transition "from a cold, imperious style to simplicity and naturalness, from amorality to a new morality, from the spirit of class division to humanity."

These ideas, which forced the violent upheaval in 1789 and

brought about the fall of entire states, were already in the making in the decade in which Bach wrote his *Well-Tempered Clavier* (Book I). The old laws are still in force, but they no longer excite the world; the new period first heralds itself; it is a kind of calm, a breath before the storm, which will soon break loose and drag with it first art, then science, then society, and finally the state. In *The Well-Tempered Clavier* Bach made good use of the old forms of prelude and fugue, but in what new ways he used them! It is his position astride the styles which gives *The Well-Tempered Clavier* its special charm, a human warmth which lets us forget the distance of more than 200 years. This we will try to show in the remaining pages of the Introduction by way of the form of the preludes and fugues, their inter-connection, their texture, harmony and elements of musical expression (tempo, dynamics, articulation, ornamentation).

The Preludes

The earliest form of the instrumental prelude is the player's improvisatory tuning of his instrument, as it is still practiced today in the music of the Orient. In the sixteenth century these introductions took more definite forms, were written down, and were called *präambulum* or *intonatio*. They were not given inde-pendent musical significance. Only after 1600 do we see how various forms of preludes were developed in suitable and different categories of music. One such special form was the organ prelude for the sacred service; oratorios and cantatas required instrumental introductions; in the opera two chief types of prelude were quickly distinguished: the French over-ture and the Italian sinfonia. The chamber sonatas of the end of the seventeenth century preceded their fugued allegro move-ments with a slow introduction, a form which was also carried over to the suite. Only one thing is still lacking in the seven-teenth century: the self-contained duality of prelude and fugue, a double form which Bach brought to its highest bloom, and which we often therefore regard as an inevitable entity, whereas it was only the culmination of a development. In the north German organ music before Bach and in the clavier music which derived from it, prelude and fugue flowed together in a single total form (the organ works of Buxtehude erroneously carry the designation "Prelude and Fugue"). Only after 1700 are the two gradually separated, become clearly distinct from one another. The earliest example of a collection of preludes and fugues is the already mentioned *Ariadne musica* by Johann Kaspar Ferdinand Fischer. In its arrangement of keys (from C Major to B Minor rising chromatically) it was also a model for Bach. Although the technique, form, and scope of the preludes and fughettas are modest, we see that in some of the preludes Fischer has already given up the old-style type of prelude, made up of scale passages and broken harmonies, and written expressive arioso-type little preludes complete in themselves. In *The Well-Tempered Clavier*, Bach copied the forms of the *Ariadne musica*, but the richness of treatment of his twenty-four[1] preludes is a constant source of astonishment. In those preludes taken from the *Klavierbüchlein für Wilhelm Friedemann Bach*, the preludes in the older style are predominant (C Major, C Minor, C Sharp Major, D Major, D Minor, also G Major and B Flat Major); others are two-part inventions (F Major, F Sharp Major, F Sharp Minor, A Minor – the last two with some freely added notes); three-part inventions are also encountered (E Major, G Sharp Minor, A Major, B Major). To those are added arioso pieces such as the Preludes in C Sharp Minor, E Flat Minor, E Minor (first part), F Minor, G Minor, B Flat Minor. The Prelude in A Flat Major is a small concerto movement, the Prelude in B Minor a two-part pre-Classic sonata movement. Taken all in all, the preludes here show a greater variety than those in the suites which precede the allemandes, courantes and other dance movements. In the process many of the preludes are raised to individual prominence; they no longer need the fugue, but from their relationship with it they gain a new reflected significance.

The Interconnection of Prelude and Fugue

It is a necessary requirement for every cyclic work that its parts (movements) must, notwithstanding their self-sufficiency,

---

[1] Keller here speaks of Book I of *The Well-Tempered Clavier* as though he had no further intent of completing his analysis of Book II. This is also to be noted occasionally elsewhere. Fortunately, this book was expanded in conception to include the whole of the 48. – Tr.

achieve a higher unity in the whole work, whether they be movements of a suite, concerto, sonata or symphony, or whether they be a prelude and fugue. This necessity is accomplished in a great variety of ways in different types of works. In the organ forms of Buxtehude and his contemporaries, the unity is so great that it would be impossible to pry apart the toccata-like and fugue sections which make up a whole. But as prelude and fugue became separated from one another, the same tonality was at first the only common bond. With Buxtehude (and also in Bach's Organ Toccata in D Minor, BWV 565) the fugue subject was built from motives of the introductory toccata. One might derive a relationship of this sort from tradition, rather than giving it the deeper meaning of an inner connection. This relationship naturally could be credible without motivic connection: a prelude serves as a preparation for a fugue, a connection which we feel in almost all of the preludes and fugues of *The Well-Tempered Clavier*, without having to demonstrate it or prove it. Where Bach found the connection unsatisfactory, in the preludes included from the *Klavierbüchlein für Wilhelm Friedemann Bach*, he added a concluding climactic passage, which lead directly to the fugue: examples are[1] the preludes in C Minor, C Sharp Minor, D Major, D Minor, E Minor, F Minor. Equally close is the connection with the preludes in C Major, C Sharp Major, F Major, F Sharp Major, F Sharp Minor, G Minor, A Flat Major, B Flat Major, B Flat Minor, B Major and B Minor; it is weaker with those preludes which, through their forms, have relinquished the character of a prelude, as in the preludes in G Sharp Minor and A Major, which one can designate as three-part inventions, weaker still in those preludes and fugues which were only connected with one another as an afterthought, as in the preludes and fugues in E Flat Major and A Minor. (That the prelude in E Flat Minor and the fugue in D Sharp Minor could grow to an ideal unity counts as a stroke of good luck.) Moreover in a number of cases motivic relationships can be demonstrated between the preludes and fugues: in C Major, C Minor, D Major, F Sharp Major, F Sharp Minor, G Major, B Flat Major, B Major, B Minor, also less strongly in C Sharp Major, C Sharp Minor, F Minor, G Minor, A Flat Major but scarcely in D Minor,

[1] In Book I. – Tr.

E Flat Minor, F Major, G Sharp Minor, and not at all in E Flat Major, E Major, A Major, A Minor and B Flat Minor.[1] In our time Wilhelm Werker and Johann Nepomuk David have concerned themselves particularly with demonstrating a motivic relationship between all the preludes and their fugues, Werker for the first 12 numbers of Book I, David for all 48. Werker's daring constructions crumbled immediately at the first critic's attack (Arnold Schering in the *Bach-Jahrbuch* 1923). David had tried to find individual notes of the fugue subject in individual notes of the prelude, unconcerned about whether those notes were main melody notes or unaccented neighboring tones; this attempt too was fairly generally rejected, as much for its extension to all the pieces of *The Well-Tempered Clavier* as for its method. Nevertheless, research must thank both men for many clarifications of previously unforeseen relationships. The problem cannot be handled summarily, but only in individual discussions of the preludes and fugues. That ideas originating and developing in the prelude have an effect on the mind of the composer is almost self-evident; yet their transformation may be so deeply rooted that it can no longer be demonstrated analytically.

The Fugues

With Bach, not only the prelude, but also the fugue arrives at the culmination of a long history. Detailing that history here will, however, be avoided; in its place will be, for the reader not formally tutored in music, some discussion of the nature, form and terminology of the fugue.

The Subject

Since the fugue consists of the statement and development of a single subject, this subject must have special characteristics. Certain limitations placed upon the subject are explained by the vocal origin of the fugue in the motets and mass movements of the fifteenth and sixteenth centuries: it must begin on the tonic or the fifth of the key; it must build a coherent line, not falling apart into thesis and antithesis. It should not

[1] In Book I. – Tr.

exceed the compass of an octave. It enters in one voice (thus every layman recognizes the fugue). The second entry, because it follows the first voice, was called *comes* (companion), while the first voice was. called *dux* (leader). The third voice enters again in the tonic as *dux*, the fourth (if the fugue is four-part) as *comes*. In *The Well-Tempered Clavier*[1] there are eleven three-part fugues, ten four-part, two five-part and one two-part. The initial consecutive entrances of the voices is called the exposition. In *The Well-Tempered Clavier*[2] the exposition in three fugues (C Major, F Minor, F Sharp Minor) is irregular with respect to the order of the *dux* and *comes*.

After 1700 the subject was also permitted a modulation to the dominant. Five subjects in *The Well-Tempered Clavier* (Book I) made use of this (E Flat Major, E Minor, G Sharp Minor, A Major and B Minor; with the E Major, opinions vary as to where the subject ends). If the *dux* modulates to the dominant, the *comes* returns to the tonic, a rule to which only the Fugue in E Minor makes an exception.

Real and Tonal Answers

If the *comes* transposes the subject note for note into the dominant, it is called a real answer. In the older music up to and including Bach, it was the rule that the fifth of the key (thus in C Major: G) should be answered not with its own fifth, but with the octave (thus G not with D′ but with C′). This was valid only indeed for the beginning of the subject; it had the purpose of closely linking the *comes* tonally to the *dux*; a key should not be left immediately at the outset.

[1] In Book I. – Tr.   [2] In Book I. – Tr.

Consequently the *comes* was altered but only in regard to the one questionable note, while the continuation was the same as in a real answer. The examples may make that clear.

In *The Well-Tempered Clavier* with the exception of the E Minor Fugue all of the subjects are answered tonally.[1] If the fifth of the key does not appear at the beginning of the subject (as for example in the subject of the C Major Fugue), the distinction between real and tonal responses disappears.

Countersubject

Countersubject means countermelody, counterpoint (*punctus contra punctum*); in the fugue it is the counterpoint to the subject appearing simultaneously with the *comes*. In the course of the fugue it can change or be retained (regular countersubject); in *The Well-Tempered Clavier* regular countersubjects predominate in order that the unity of the fugue may be more strongly emphasized. Bach indeed goes further in that he often takes the material for the countersubject from the subject itself. In several fugues the subject is accompanied by two regular countersubjects (for example,[2] C Minor, C Sharp Major, F Minor, B Flat Major).

Exposition

The consecutive uninterrupted entry of all the voices one after another is called a complete exposition of the subject; should

[1] There is considerable room for interpretation here. The C Major Fugue, essentially a stretto-fugue, is a case in point, although as Keller observes, the fifth does not appear at the beginning of the subject. I would personally describe the answers to the fugue subjects of the F Sharp Minor, the G Major and A Minor Fugues of Book I, for example, as real rather than tonal. In Book II, an even larger number have real answers: the C Sharp Minor, D Minor, D Sharp Minor, E Minor, F Sharp Major, G Sharp Minor and B Flat Minor fugues, in some of which the fifth does indeed appear late. The E Major, A Major and B Major fugues of Book II represent special cases in which the fifth is never touched (in the E Major, the subject does not reach that far; in the B Major, there is a charming conspiracy to avoid it) or touched only in passing at the end of the subject. In every case, one understands the musical grounds on which the real response was preferred by Bach; in some instances a tonal answer is conceivable.—Tr.
[2] In Book I.—Tr.

a voice be missing, the exposition is incomplete. After the first entry of all the voices (the exposition) the movement is carried further, the lines are spun out occasionally with still an extra entry of one other voice; at the same time there will be a modulation into one of the most closely related keys, in the major chiefly to the dominant, in the minor similarly or to the relative major key. How many expositions[1] a fugue may contain is dependent upon the subject and what the composer wishes to develop from it. According to the "school" rule, a fugue should contain three expositions; however there are in *The Well-Tempered Clavier* numerous deviations from the rule: in Book I the F Sharp Minor Fugue contains only two, the E Flat Minor Fugue six expositions. The normal course of a fugue leads to the dominant and returns to the tonic by way of the subdominant. As to detailed procedures, there are no fast rules as there are in sonata or rondo form of the Viennese classics. Fugue is therefore, on the one hand, in its limitations upon one subject and given number of voices, the most rigid of musical forms, yet, in the working out of its subject, the freest. In many fugues in *The Well-Tempered Clavier* after the initial exposition there is no further complete exposition of all the voices. Often the entries lie so far from one another that only forcibly can they be brought together into the conception of an exposition.

Episodes

The connecting passages between two expositions are called episodes. Their main function is to prepare for the next entry of the subject, but particularly to relax the form. For this purpose sequences whose material has been taken from the subject through transformation are chiefly used. Here also

---

[1] Where the German word "*Durchführung*" should be translated as exposition and where as re-exposition has given the translator some problems. The German word also means "development," although that does not add to the confusion here. In English we distinguish the first exposition from subsequent expositions by calling the latter "re-expositions" however artificial the distinction. Here is a typical example of the problem: in referring to the E Flat Minor Fugue of Book I, I have spoken of "six expositions" rather than of an opening exposition and five re-expositions. – Tr.

there is no fast rule. In some fugues ([in Book I] for example the first one in C Major) there are scarcely any episodes; in others (for example in C Minor, E Flat Major, F Minor, G Major and others) the episodes appear almost autonomous and as contrasts to the subject.

Devices of Fugue

These concern not only the subject but also its development. The subject may, in the course of the fugue, enter in inversion (in *The Well-Tempered Clavier* [Book I] this is the case with the fugues in D Minor, E Flat Minor, F Sharp Minor, G Major, A Minor and B Major), or in augmentation, that is in double note values (E Flat Minor Fugue), and it can be used with another voice in stretto, that is overlapped with it. Not every subject permits stretto; where it happens however it reinforces the strength, and for this reason in many fugues this artistic device is reserved for the final climax. Bach makes very frequent use of stretto, in *The Well-Tempered Clavier* [Book I] in the fugues in C Major, C Sharp Minor, D Major, D Minor, E Flat Minor, F Major, G Major, G Minor, A Major, A Minor and B Flat Minor. In the stretto, the intervallic distance of the two voice entries is as important as the time distance. The most frequent interval, because easiest to grasp and to manipulate, is the octave; after it, the fifth and the fourth; other intervals are more rare because they alter the harmonic sense of the subject too much. The time distance is usually a half measure. If it is shorter, the first voice treads, so to say, on the heels of the second; with wider time distances the stretto is no longer an art. That the final climax of a fugue is often introduced by an organpoint on the dominant, or that it may run itself out on a tonic organpoint happens frequently and is of great effect, but it does not belong to the essence of fugue.

Double and Triple Fugues

A fugue with two subjects is called a double fugue. There are two types to distinguish: the first, the only type used in older music, combines from the beginning two subjects into a double subject, and develops them in this relationship through the whole fugue. In Book I of *The Well-Tempered Clavier* this type is no longer encountered. The second type first develops the first subject, then the second subject by itself alone, and combines both in a final section. This more effective type indeed does not yet appear in the first part of *The Well-Tempered Clavier*, but appears several times in the second part. There are several possibilities for a fugue with three themes (a great rarity in music) of which in Book I the C Sharp Minor Fugue, in Book II the F Sharp Minor Fugue serve as examples.

This survey has shown how many possibilities the fugue offers the composer. The variety of fugues in *The Well-Tempered Clavier* is almost inexhaustible, every subject has its own character, it has a distinct individuality through which the form and technique of fugue composition unfold. The treatment of the subject varies from fugue to fugue; each develops in its own manner the strengths enclosed within the subject. Even a subject of a few notes can encompass powerful forces, which in the course of the fugue are set free (C Sharp Minor Fugue [Book I – Tr.]). Others are based on a richly subdivided subject, which the fugue contrives to give a new appearance at each entry: ([in Book I – Tr.] Fugues in C Sharp Major, E Flat Major, F Sharp Major, B Flat Major).

In *The Well-Tempered Clavier* one can distinguish subjects invented vocally or instrumentally. Purely vocal [in Book I] are the subjects of the fugues in C Sharp Minor, E Flat Minor, F Minor, F Sharp Minor, A Flat Major, B Flat Minor; vocal with instrumental modifications (or influences), typical of many of Bach's choral fugues, are those in C Major, D Minor, F Major, G Minor, B Major, B Minor; purely instrumentally invented – and therefore in their character the most modern – are the fugue subjects in C Minor, C Sharp Major, D Major, E Flat Major, E Major, E Minor, F Sharp Major, G Major, G Sharp Minor, A Major, A Minor and B Flat Major. In my book *Die Klavierwerke Bachs* (The Clavier Works of Bach) I designated these opposing types as "concentrated" and "relaxed" forms.[1] From what has been said it is apparent that

[1] The fugues are not only to be classified as vocally or instrumentally based, but might indeed be indicated as deriving either from the *canzona* or *ricercare*, as the case may be. The *canzona*-type fugues are more frequently

formal, school-type analysis of the fugues of *The Well-Tempered Clavier* can tell us little about their nature and their significance. Too deep an invasion into the living organism of a work of art can be lethal, especially if the implements of dissection are blunt – and if this attempt be made with preconceived conceptions derived from theoretical instruction.

In the instrumentally formed subjects and fugues of *The Well-Tempered Clavier* was the seed of a future development of fugue which never came to fruition because the generation after Bach turned to other goals. In both the Viennese classic as well as the Romantic periods, the fugue was conceived as a venerable, somewhat pedantic form and was handled in a conservative sense; only Beethoven went further than Bach in his giant fugues in Opus 106 and 133. He was followed by Julius Reubke (Organ Sonata on the Ninety-fourth Psalm), Liszt (B–A–C–H), César Franck (Prelude, Chorale and Fugue) and others. They brought fresh life to the fugue, which in our time has experienced a rich second blooming through Max Reger, Paul Hindemith, D. Shostakovitch and others.

Notation

The appearance of the notes has a specific suggestive effect upon the player. Whether the composer prescribes large or small measures, whether the eighth note or the sixteenth note is the smallest note value, whether he uses small or large beams, whether he places a fermata on the final chord or the double bar after it, indeed, whether he notates a middle voice in the upper or lower staff, adds to the impression which the music carries to the player through the medium of the appearance of the notes.

The autograph, the copies and the oldest printings of *The Well-Tempered Clavier* contain only the pure text of the notes, without the addition of tempo marks, without dynamics or other designation, without signs of articulation (slurs, wedges, dots). The upper staff is notated in the soprano clef as was the custom about 1740 (only No. 17 in Book II makes an excep-

---

in three voices (or in one instance, only two); the *ricercare*-type fugues are more likely to be in four voices or even five. – Tr.

tion, for special reasons). Bach does not change to other clefs (alto, mezzo-soprano, tenor clef) – which Friedemann still had to learn in the introduction to the *Klavierbüchlein* – perhaps out of consideration for the "young, eager-to-learn," who no longer knew them. The basic metric unit of most preludes and fugues is the quarter note divided into sixteenths. Where only eighth and quarter notes are used, a reference to the older style is indicated (the Prelude in B Minor, the Fugues in E Flat Minor and F Sharp Minor); where only half and quarter notes are used, a further retrogression to the old vocal style (fugues in B Flat Minor in Book I and E Major in Book II); where thirty-second notes take the place of sixteenth notes, a diminution of the form (Prelude in B Flat Major).[1] Triple-meter measures are treated similarly: [in Book I] the F Sharp Major prelude shows its tenderness and intimacy through the fact that it is written not in 6/8 but 6/16 meter; the C Sharp Minor Prelude stands in 6/4, not 6/8 meter as a prelude to its fugue. Small measures transmit the impression of agility, nimbleness; the C Sharp Major Prelude would lose something if it were notated in 6/8 or 12/8 meter. Large measures convey the feeling of spaciousness, of inner peace: in the 3/2 meter of the E Flat Minor Prelude in Book I, of the F Major Prelude in Book II, in the 4/2 meter of the E Major Fugue in Book II. The fugues in F Major in Book I and B Minor in Book II are in 3/8 meter because they have the character of a *passepied* which always appeared in 3/8 meter, while the formal minuet preferred the 3/4 meter, and so on.

In Bach's time the dot did not always have the significance of a lengthening of a note value by one-half. For that reason ♪.♬ for the most part signifies ♪♬: only later (in Book II, No. 17) did Bach notate precisely.

In the French overture the dot was, at the discretion of the player, often sharpened to a double dot (Goethe heard in this sharp punctuation the rapping of the staff of the Master of Ceremonies); however such freedoms were omitted in polyphonic movements.

[1] Book I. – Tr.

Endings

In older music a movement always ended with a wholenote or a double wholenote. That is normal also with Bach. However with him we already find endings on unaccented parts of the measure (Prelude in F Sharp Major in Book I), and others which break off abruptly (E Minor Fugue in Book I), or let the voices disappear as if evaporating (Prelude in F Major in Book I).

The visual sign for the close was the fermata, the *"corona"*, which lay protectively over the final chord. Bach made more distinctions. In certain cases the fermata is missing (in Book I, the Fugue in C Minor, the Preludes in C Sharp Major, C Sharp Minor and A Minor); in several cases it stands over the double bar in order to emphasize the effect of the close without its being held longer (Preludes in E Major, E Minor, F Sharp Major, B Minor, Fugues in F Sharp Minor and G Major); to emphasize this ending still more, Bach occasionally writes two fermatas, one over the final note, one over the double bar (Preludes in D Minor, G Minor, A Major, B Major; Fugues in A Minor, B Flat Minor, B Minor).

It was obvious that a movement could conclude only on the tonic note or its octave. That is still today the most frequent case; but Bach was one of the first to recognize the charm of a closing on the third (Prelude and Fugue in C Minor, Fugue in B Major in Book I, Fugues in C Sharp Major and G Major in Book II).

Before Bach's time it was the rule to end minor movements in the major, for the consonance of the minor triad was considered unsatisfactory for a conclusion. Only with the music of Viennese classic did the shift to the major signify a desired sudden change (Beethoven, Symphonies No. 5 and 9, final movements). The transition took place in Bach's lifetime. In organ and church works he usually retains the major ending (a magnificent exception is the Organ Toccata in D Minor, BWV 565); in his suites and partitas he frequently concludes in minor. In *The Well-Tempered Clavier* he is more conservative: in Book I he concludes only the G Sharp Minor Fugue in minor; in Book II there are as many as six such movements (the Preludes in C Minor, C Sharp Minor, D Sharp Minor, F Minor, G Sharp Minor and the Fugue in C Minor).

Harmony and Texture

Bach's harmony was built on the firm foundation of thorough-bass harmony. Such harmony consists of the connection of triads on the steps of the scale and seventh chords in major and minor with a few alterations and with modulations to the nearest related keys. These modulations are carried out for the most part diatonically, occasionally chromatically, very rarely enharmonically. Bach seldom exceeds these limits; in *The Well-Tempered Clavier*, not at all. Nowhere is there an enharmonic change (as for example in the *Sarabande* of the Third English Suite, BWV 808); rare are chromatic shifts as at the end of the D Minor Prelude [Book I]; when indeed chromaticism enters (the subjects of the Fugues in F Minor and B Minor), it is used functionally. When Beethoven spoke of Bach as the "father of harmony" he meant by "harmony" many-voicedness, polyphony.[1] The dissonances of Bach arise almost always through the collision of two voices. As dissonant sound combinations he knew only the diminished seventh chord and the Neapolitan sixth chord, and even these play no great role in *The Well-Tempered Clavier*. As harmonist, Bach in *The Well-Tempered Clavier* is an intentional conservative, "well-tempered" (at the opposite pole lies the Chromatic Fantasy, BWV 903, written at about the same time).

The texture of the fugues is naturally conditioned by the laws of fugue; accompanying voices may never sink to bare harmonic accompaniment; also in the episodes every voice must preserve its own life, its own significance. The texture of the preludes is freer. But even the preludes often limit themselves to a given number of voices. For two voices (in Book I) there are the preludes in F Major, F Sharp Major, G Major, and with certain additional notes also the G Sharp Major, D Major, D Minor, F Sharp Minor; three voices: G Minor, C Sharp Minor, A Major, B Major, B Minor; four voices: E Flat Major, and F Minor; five voices: B Flat Minor. More diverse is the texture in the preludes in C Minor, E Flat Minor, A Flat Major, and B Flat Major and in E Minor; the single-

---

[1] It is not quite so certain to me that this is what Beethoven had in mind: certainly the Bach of the chorale harmonizations, familiar to every harmony student, has also synthesized harmonic practice for us. – Tr.

voiced C Major Prelude is a figuration of a truly five-voiced texture. In the three-voiced fugues, and in certain preludes, the middle voice takes on sometimes the significance of an alto, sometimes of a tenor; the bottom voice, too, is not always a bass, but occasionally has tenor characteristics.

Tempo

With the exception of No. 24 (B Minor) and the preludes in C Minor and E Minor, Book I lacks any indication of tempo; in Book II only the preludes in G Minor and B Minor have tempo indications. Bach used such indications only in chamber music; in music for an individual player (organ, clavier) he could rely upon the player's knowledge of the style. The "*Tempo ordinario*" of the Baroque was an *Allegro molto moderato*, corresponding to the measured, controlled bearing of a man of position; the limits above and below it were narrower than in the Viennese classic style. Often the smallest note values or the ornaments give information on the tempo, more naturally still the "*Affekt*" of each piece. Thus the style of the period, Bach's personal style, and the individual style of every single piece operate jointly and must be taken into account by the player. Occurring within very narrow limits, even small tempo variations are of significance for performance. Decisive for the tempo is the metric unit, the pulse beat of a piece. Smaller metric units than the quarter occur in *The Well-Tempered Clavier* only once: in the A Minor Prelude in Book II; larger metric units naturally occur with the tempo indication c, which does not always indicate an especially lively tempo, but often is only characteristic of the older style. The obituary of Bach recorded: "In conducting he was very accurate and in tempo, which he normally kept very lively, entirely secure." That describes the choleric Bach, but it is to be understood only within the narrower boundaries of the Baroque.

The tempo ought thus not be changed within a movement, with the obvious exception of a *ritardando* before the close. When this should begin and how strongly it should hold back the movement is dependent entirely upon the individual case. It can also be omitted entirely, [in Book I] perhaps at the end of the Preludes in C Sharp Major, E Major, and F Major, F Sharp

Major and others, but it is indispensable before fermatas (Preludes in B Flat Minor in the first volume and F Sharp Minor in the second volume, the Fugues in A Minor in the first volume and E Minor in the second). Also a change of tempo prescribed by Bach within a piece must be suitably prepared (Preludes in C Minor and E Minor, Book I). At the end of the discussion of individual preludes and fugues I have suggested metronome markings which naturally should not be considered obligatory, but can be modified by every player according to his own temperament. According to Walter Gerstenberg, the tempos of the preludes and fugues should stand in simple rational numerical relationship to each other; I have borne this in mind as far as possible in the suggested metronome markings.

Dynamics

Since Bach intended the preludes and fugues of *The Well-Tempered Clavier* for a single-manual keyboard instrument, he needed to prescribe no dynamic markings; for, even on the harpsichord, no register should be added or subtracted in the course of a single piece. Only the G Sharp Minor Prelude in Book II has in one place the notation "*piano*" for an echo-like repetition, "*forte*" for the return to the first dynamic level. Consequently a pianist must decide for every prelude or fugue upon a basic timbre and dynamic level which he may modify thoughtfully, but not abandon. The two chief sins of Czerny against *The Well-Tempered Clavier* were his often senselessly rapid metronome markings and the use of all the gradations of tone which the piano permits. Relics of this conception are still to be encountered today here and there, but no one would any longer conclude the G Sharp Minor Fugue after a *fortissimo* climax with a gradual *diminuendo* to *pianissimo*. We are (or were) rather in the danger of falling into the opposite extreme: to perform Bach soullessly, "mechanistically" one might call it. Then all is lost of the "*cantable Art im Spielen*" (the cantabile manner of playing) which Bach regarded as the most important thing. The climaxes at the end of the Preludes in C Minor, D Major, D Minor, B Flat Minor are unthinkable on the piano without (gradual) dynamic intensifications; equally improbably can one get from the first part of the E Minor Prelude to the second part without a *crescendo* from *piano* to *forte*. One must guard as much against a styleless use of the dynamic practice of Beethoven and of the nineteenth century as against a timid historicism.

Phrasing and Articulation

In no area are music and speech so closely bound together, and no area is hence so important for thoughtful performance as that of phrasing and articulation. In my work *Die Musikalische Artikulation, besonders bei J. S. Bach* (1925) and in its broader new version, *Phrasierung und Artikulation . . .* (1954)[1] I have dealt with both areas exhaustively and delineated them from each other. Phrasing is the study of musically connected ideas, it is concerned with the interrelationship of thoughts ("what I am saying"); articulation is not involved in the interrelationship of thoughts, but it gives to thought, through *legato* and *staccato*, with all the steps between, life and color ("how I say it"). The components are the same as in words; but whereas with the written word the sense is made visible to the eye through the phrase signs (punctuation), composers, with very few exceptions, have declined to make the phrasing recognizable on the musical page. In the forms which derive from song and dance it is not difficult to find the correct phrasing; for the most part it reveals itself. It is more difficult in the forms of music which derive from prose, most difficult of all in polyphonic music in which every voice has its own life. In a fugue the performer is advised to phrase every voice through separately, in sections. The limit of a phrase is generally the limit of breath; where the singer must take a breath, a phrase ending can be made. Often the phrases are inter-linked so that a caesura is not possible, as for example in many fugues at the point of transition from subject into countersubject. He who "phrases" too much or too arbitrarily is in the danger of fragmenting Bach's overall line.

In *The Well-Tempered Clavier* (with very few exceptions) Bach also did not give any indication of the articulation. Natural

---

[1] Translated by the present translator and published by W. W. Norton, 1965, in the USA; by Barrie & Rockliff in England, 1966. A paperback version with new preface was brought out by Norton in 1973.

articulation consists of binding together narrow intervals (seconds); of slightly separating the notes of middle-sized intervals (fourths and fifths) from one another; and of separating distinctly large intervals, those which can only be reached through a "leap." As a normal instance of natural articulation consider, for example, the subject of the first fugue of *The Well-Tempered Clavier*. It may also be the case that the inner cohesion of thought requires a continual legato, as with the theme of the F Minor Fugue in Book I; and it is equally possible to relax a line that consists of scalewise steps with *staccato* (perhaps the countersubject of the C Minor Fugue, Book I). The possibilities of articulation are inexhaustible. Carl Philipp Emanuel Bach says about it in his *Versuch über die wahre Art, das Clavier zu spielen*: ... "One must separate notes with a difference, and must ponder the value of the note, whether it be half a bar, a quarter note or an eighth, whether the tempo be brisk or slow, whether the intent be *forte* or *piano*; such notes[1] are always held somewhat less than half their value. In general, one can say that separation occurs more frequently in notes that leap and in rapid tempos." That is well worth taking to heart, yet we are familiar with still more degrees of the *staccato* on our present-day instruments. With quarter notes, a shortening by a sixteenth or even less is effective as a clear separation.

Ornamentation

The significance of ornamentation as an integral part of Bach's tonal art was first fully recognized only in our time; we see in Bach's ornamentation no longer fashionable "beauty spots" which one might prefer to wish were not there. It is, however, of importance to observe where and in what way Bach uses his ornaments. They are found in greatest profusion in the ornamented *cantus firmi* of organ chorales: next, in the *Sarabandes* of the Suites ("*Les Agréments de la même Sarabande*"), and in certain very early works (Capriccio on the Departure of his Beloved Brother, bwv 992, and others). In his later work we see Bach striving for a spiritualization of the ornaments. These are now

---

[1] 'Such notes': 'indicated either by means of a small stroke or through dots set over them' as C. P. E. Bach states in a passage preceding this. – Tr.

often completely written out as in the middle movement of the Italian Concerto (BWV 971) and Variation 25 of the Goldberg Variations (BWV 988).

The Well-Tempered Clavier is adorned with ornaments in a strikingly sparing manner. In many preludes and fugues there is no ornamentation whatsoever, in others only the usual trill on the penultimate note. Only the arioso preludes are treated more richly: C Sharp Minor (here the ornaments were added afterwards), E Flat Minor and E Minor (first half). Longer trills are found only in the preludes in F Major, F Sharp Major and G Minor. Rarely is there a mordent, a turn only in the D Minor Fugue in Book I; the theme of the C Minor Fugue in Book I contains a written-out mordent, the G Major Fugue in Book I, a written-out turn. For this Bach was scolded. "All the grace notes, all the little ornaments and everything which one understands should be played according to the conventions he writes out with the notes themselves, and that takes away from his pieces not only the beauty of the harmony, but it makes the melody throughout indiscernible" was the judgment of Scheibe in 1737 in the "*Critischer Musikus*." It is evident that Bach, when he played his own things, introduced ornaments *ex tempore*, a right which the present-day player may also assume (naturally the old instruments permit more ornaments than does our piano). As regards the performance of the trill, all the theorists of the period taught that it ought to begin with the upper neighboring note. Practice, however, also permitted beginning in certain cases with the chief note. Trills always begin with the upper neighbor where, instead of the given note, there could be an appoggiatura. Trills which begin with the chief note are 1) those of the organpoint type, especially in the bass; 2) where a repetition of a note should be avoided (the subject of the F Sharp Major Fugue in Book I); and 3) where a trill begins without preparation (F Sharp Major Fugue, Book II). An ornament is a decoration; how much decoration one will apply, taste decides. Nowhere is pedantic narrow-mindedness so little in place as here.

These observations, which concern all of the preludes and fugues of *The Well-Tempered Clavier*, conclude this Introduction (in which the questions raised could naturally only be dealt with in succinct brevity). We now turn our attention to the individual preludes and fugues. Therein measure numbers cannot be avoided and the reader is asked to place a copy of *The Well-Tempered Clavier* by his side and to read along with it. The author does not believe that today a measure-by-measure progressive description ("analysis") of the course of a prelude or a fugue is necessary as Riemann still held; whoever plays *The Well-Tempered Clavier* can do this for himself; but he should be made aware of what gives the special character to each piece. Whereas all merely formal analyses are, and must be, more or less schematic, here the individual traits which give *The Well-Tempered Clavier* its extraordinary "variety in its unity" will be brought to the fore.

Book I
bwv 846–869

The key of C Major has many faces: in its neutrality it can serve equally well a Czerny study or Mozart's Jupiter Symphony (KV 551) or Wagner's Prelude to *Die Meistersinger*. In the first piece of *The Well-Tempered Clavier* it has the charm of the unspoken, of the "ominous" as the young Goethe might have said. From broken harmonies, this prelude weaves a curtain before the fugue which, with a certain spiritual sobriety, takes the player immediately under strict discipline.

The Prelude

On a keyboard instrument, to prelude in broken harmonies was the general practice of the time. Often the composer gave only a harmonic sketch which the player could realize as he saw fit; Handel's clavier pieces offer numerous examples of this, and Bach himself did likewise in the introduction to the great Fugue in A Minor (BWV 944) and in the arpeggios of the *Chromatic Fantasy*. But Bach wrote out fully the little Prelude in C Minor *"pour le luth"* (BWV 999) and the first prelude of *The Well-Tempered Clavier*. Harmonically considered, this work holds only a single cadence in C Major, expanded through secondary dominants; the eight measures of organpoint on G correspond to the four on C at the close. However, Bach offers more than broken chords; in them is hidden a truly five-voiced movement in which every four measures taken together create one larger measure:

In only one place is the four-measure grouping relaxed: measures 21–23 create a three-measure group, occasioned by the chromatic compression of the bass:

This irregularity was noticed by one annotator (Schwencke), who inserted a measure after bar 22 in order to standardize the meter:

Schwencke was an educated, well-informed musician, who did not intend to "improve" upon Bach; but the so-called "Schwencke measure" was adopted in the nineteenth century by a whole series of editions.

We know two early forms of this prelude. The first, handed down by Forkel, numbers 23 measures (or, if one counts the final measure as doubled, 24). It does not contain the characteristic upper melody line of the later conception:

The second, included in the *Klavierbüchlein für Wilhelm Friedemann Bach*, numbers 27 (28) measures (BWV 846a):

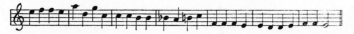

In the final version in *The Well-Tempered Clavier*, the metrical accentuations have been changed once more and the prelude expanded through the two organpoints to 35 (36) measures:

Wilhelm Werker was the first to point out that the upper melody line of the beginning (e″–f″–e″–a″–d″–g″) quite clearly anticipates the fugue subject; Johann Nepomuk David made us aware that this prelude, although confined to the key of C Major without modulation, manages to include all of the 12 semitones strewn through it as an announcement (understandable only to the initiated) of the route through all 12 scale degrees on which we are about to embark.

It conceals within itself a profusion of possibilities for performance. Gounod made it the basis for his *Ave Maria*, a religious meditation – the time when this romanticized eccentricity was popular is past, but opinions concerning the prelude's proper performance are still greatly varied. On the harpsichord the author suggests playing the prelude with an eightfoot stop without change of manual (as Schweitzer proposed); on the piano in a quiet tempo, neither lively nor slow, "*semplice*" and without a great climax, without pedal (in order not to destroy the pedal effect envisaged by Bach in the first two notes), as a prelude[1] which opens up the way into the fugue and allegorically into the whole work. Quarter note equals 72.

The Fugue à 4

What the prelude lets us glimpse as through a veil lies open to view in this fugue; it fulfils what the prelude promised. It is a "proving ground," as someone said in Bach's time, in the same way as the first two-part invention serves as a model of how "not only to write good inventions, but also to develop them well." To be successful in the eyes of a scholar, a fugue subject must conform to traditional forms while showing unmistakably the personal handwriting of the composer. Both elements are present in the subject of this first fugue. Its archetype is the hexachord rising from the tonic and returning again, a model much used in the seventeenth century and on which Bach wrote an imperfect youthful fugue (BWV 946). In

[1] Here Keller writes "*Vor-Spiel*," which is to say "pre-play." – Tr.

Weimar he also based the subject of an organ fugue on a segment of the hexachord (BWV 545):

Here one can see an earlier form of the subject developed in *The Well-Tempered Clavier,* and at the same time recognize the basic difference between fugue subjects for organ and clavier: the organ subject is rooted firmly and clearly on the accented parts of the measure. The clavier subject however begins with an eighth rest, giving the whole first measure an upbeat significance and weakening the accent on d′ in the next bar. Moreover, Bach gives a feeling of ambiguity to the end of the subject by carrying the phrase past it. (Only at the alto entry in measures 9–10 does it become clear that the subject ends on e′ in the middle of the second measure.) In the autograph the subject originally had the following form:

Only later was the rhythm so sharpened through the thirty-second notes that the subject received more character and a stronger drive propelling it to the fourth and fifth. Although it consists of a single directed line, it is nevertheless constructed with remarkable symmetry; the fifth a′ to d′ serves as a middle axis separating two fourths; at the close, the falling scale passage a′ to e′ corresponds with the rising scale passage c′ to f′ at the beginning. The subject consists of fourteen notes. Friedrich Smend (*Bach bei seinem Namen gerufen* – "Bach called by his Name") has called attention to the fact that the sum of the letters of Bach's name, if one enumerates them according to their order in the alphabet, totals fourteen ($2+1+3+8 = 14$). In this way Bach may have hidden his name in the structure of his work in much the same fashion as a master architect might have done in the Middle Ages. Speculation did not end here. Werker has counted the entries of the subject. There are 24, thus a profound, hidden allusion to the 24 keys through which we shall travel in *The Well-Tempered*

Clavier. This would explain the unusual form of this first fugue. If it must include 24 entries of the subject without exceeding the compass of two written pages (in our editions two printed pages) this would only be possible through continual stretti of the subject, in which this fugue is richer than any other in *The Well-Tempered Clavier.* One entry follows upon the heels of another, so that neither time nor space remains for episodes, nor for a regular countersubject, for the subject is constantly counterpointed with itself. In the face of these limitations, Bach feels free to shape the exposition irregularly, with the order *dux–comes–comes–dux,* so that already in the first fugue we have an example of the fact that – as a theorist disapprovingly observed – no fugue in *The Well-Tempered Clavier* corresponds to the school-rules.

Riemann tried to establish three-part form as the rule for the fugues of *The Well-Tempered Clavier*; but here at once (and not for the last time) we have a two-part structure: its only emphasized close comes halfway (that in A Minor in measure 14). In the first half the exposition is followed by two incomplete expositions, each of three voices (beginning in measures 7 and 10). A compressed stretto of all four voices opens the second half; then the voices thin out, to thicken again in the coda (measures 24–27), at the end of which the soprano reaches, for the first and only time, c''' as the highest note. The stretti are of various types: in the first half, only at the fifth (or at the fourth below) at a distance of two eighth notes; in the second half, at other intervals as well and at a distance of four eighth notes (measure 15). Bach loved to let pairs of voices enter symmetrically. Thus the entry of the bass and alto in measure 10 corresponds to that of the soprano and tenor in measure 7, just as the free entry of the tenor in measure 12 corresponds to that of the alto in measure 9, the entry of the pair of voices of bass and soprano in measures 15 to the alto and tenor in measure 14; similarly in measures 16–17 and 19–20.

Performance: The performance of this fugue, a type Bach inherited from his predecessors, which seems to demand so little, requires much spiritual concentration. As already suggested, one should learn the four voices individually section after section, phrasing and articulating each one separately; the expenditure of time and attention will later greatly benefit the playing. The articulation of this subject – and consequently of the fugue – can serve as an example for many of the others: the steps of a second are linked, the fourth and fifth set apart distinctly, larger intervals clearly separated. In the stretti it is better to give some emphasis to the leading voice, allowing the second voice to fall somewhat into the background (ordinarily it is done in the reverse).[1] The performance should be quiet and unpretentious, as becomes the intellectual austerity of this fugue. Quarter note equals 54 to 58.

BOOK I: NO. 2 IN C MINOR, BWV 847

In Bach's time C Minor did not yet have the passionately tense character which the young Beethoven (and even Mozart in his late works) gave to it: it was the Dorian mode transposed down a wholetone, and for that reason was notated for a long time only with two flats in its key signature (still so in the *Klavierbüchlein für Wilhelm Friedemann Bach*). This prelude and fugue in C Minor are the most frequently played pieces in *The Well-Tempered Clavier*, a fact which can be traced back to Czerny, who thought of the fugue as a *scherzo* in Beethoven's manner, and the prelude as an *étude* for perfecting the ensemble of the two hands. That both of them are something quite different will be shown in what follows.

The Prelude

This prelude exists in a shorter version of only 27 bars in the *Klavierbüchlein für Wilhelm Friedemann Bach* where the first 24 measures are exactly the same as in *The Well-Tempered Clavier*. In this form it might well have been a study for Friedemann in the playing of two hands together without changing their

---

[1] The usual rule in stretto is to emphasize the voice which enters last, and to follow it through. For these pairs of entries, Keller is recommending the reverse. – Tr.

position or passing under the thumb. Its harmonic conception is distinctly related to the first prelude. In *The Well-Tempered Clavier*, Bach expanded it by only eleven measures, but how much happens in them! The *étude*-like character is given up, and in a passage of three bars in which the single-voiced figuration is divided between the two hands, the prelude reaches a climax. The tempo changes to "*presto*" and the main motive is placed a beat later in the bar in parallel motion of the two hands:

This precipitate movement is arrested in an *adagio* measure and flows in the original tempo, becoming gradually quieter, toward the major mode with an ending on the third. In these last measures the relationship to the fugue becomes clearer. In the figure e flat′–d′–e flat′ of the prelude, one could already see a reference to the mordent of the fugue subject; but only in the last bar of the prelude is the second measure of the fugue subject heard as well.

On the third quarter note in the bass of bar 18 there is a mistake in Kroll's edition which has been perpetuated in many other editions and recordings; the note should be B flat, not c, as the autograph clearly shows.

Performance: The player should remember that Bach changes the tempo three times in this short movement. The metronome marking of Czerny and Ruthardt (quarter note equals 144) is senseless because it permits no further intensification. As an alternative suggestion: until measure 25, *allegro moderato* (quarter note equals 84); measures 25–27 increased to quarter note equals 126; measure 33 *ritardando* to eighth note equals 63 ("*adagio*"); the last four measures begin with quarter note equals 84 and end with quarter note equals 63 (the tempo of the fugue). On the reason or necessity for *accelerando* and *ritardando* in transitions, see page 39ff. Generally in this prelude the first and ninth sixteenth notes are detached, but it is also possible to think of a small caesura after the fifth and thirteenth sixteenth notes.

The Fugue à 3

This fugue owes its extraordinary popularity with players as much to the charm of its subject as to its easy comprehensibility and transparent polyphony. Its subject, which is the only one in the two books of *The Well-Tempered Clavier* which begins on the upper octave, clings to a mordent-like motive, against which the eighth notes first rise up, g′ to a flat′, and then spring over it (d″ to g′) whereupon after an extended syncopation, the subject then descends to the third. The lower tonic note is not reached at all, except in the scale passage which links the subject and countersubject. (The accented parts of the measure show as the fundamental melodic movement the falling fourth a flat′–g′–f′–e flat′ [compare the two countersubjects].) The subject has a regular structure of $1+1+2=4$ metric units, similar to many themes of the Viennese classic school (e.g., the theme of the Minuet from the Sonatina in G Major, Opus 49, No. 2 of Beethoven). The sprightly character of the subject caused Czerny to conceive this fugue as a *scherzo* of Beethoven *sempre pp e staccato*, and thousands have performed it according to his directions. But the written-out mordents and the syncopation give it indeed a sharper profile, a humor shot through with caprice, which is intensified by the parenthetical motive

(an inversion of the scale in measure 3). The two countersubjects, which accompany the theme as satellites, have less profile.

This fugue is in everything the complete antithesis of the first one. There the subject was pure prose; here a line of verse.

Hence structurally both are completely different: in the C
Major Fugue the subject entered 24 times with stretti of all
sorts, and without episodes; the C Minor Fugue consists of
only two expositions and two separate entries, but it is richly
provided with episodes. It, too, is in two-part form (measures
1–15 and 15–31).[1] Each half includes a complete exposition and a single entry of the subject in the soprano.
In the first part this isolated entry is so inconspicuously
attached to the episode (measure 11) that one notices the
entrance of the subject only a half measure later! In the second
half the entries of the subject lie far apart from one another:
the alto enters in measure 15, the soprano in measure 20, the
bass in measure 26. The last soprano entry (measure 29) closes
the fugue triumphantly on the major third and in the process
confirms the ending of the third in the prelude.

The episodes make use of the rich material provided by the
subject, the transition motive, and the two countersubjects. The
episode of measures 5 and 6 is taken up again in measure 17,
developed in three voices, the voices exchanged in measure
19, where with cross relations a high-spirited play is carried
on. The second episode also enters twice (measures 9–11 and
22–25): the upper voices recall the chief motive of the subject,
the bass moves in scale passages; in measure 13 and 14 the
soprano inverts them while the two lower voices derive from
the countersubject. After the emphatic bass entry, the movement breaks off abruptly after the sharp dissonance of the
double suspension in measure 28.[2] This pause can be related
to the "*adagio*" measure of the prelude: but the prelude ends
thoughtfully with a dash, the fugue with an exclamation mark.
For this fugue, which is played at every piano lesson, the
Czerny conception which still exists in a host of editions,
should be replaced with one which is truer to style. This
requires a somewhat restrained tempo, a moderate degree of
loudness in place of *pp*, and an articulation according to
Bach's principles: in the subject, the mordent-like sixteenths
should be linked, the eighth notes set apart with accent, and
the syncopation on A flat prepared by two staccato sixteenths.
The notes of the transitional scales are lightly joined, the

[1] Keller has 32; there are only 31 measures. – Tr.
[2] Keller: 29. – Tr.

eighth notes of the two countersubjects lightly separated. Only varied articulation does justice to the half-jesting, half-recalcitrant character of the fugue, and only thus is the *forte* close believable. Quarter note equals 63 (as in the close of the prelude).

BOOK I: NO. 3 IN C SHARP MAJOR, BWV 848

Bach was the first to use this key with the greatest number of sharps in our music and he has remained almost the only one. Only Haydn writes, in his C Sharp Minor Sonata (Hoboken XVI: 36), the Trio of the Minuet in C Sharp Major, while Beethoven in his C Sharp Minor Sonata and Schumann in the finale of his Symphonic Etudes write in D Flat Major, just as Chopin does in the middle section of his C Sharp Minor Polonaise. The reason Bach wrote in *The Well-Tempered Clavier* in C Sharp Major and not in D Flat Major is just as simple as it is sensible: both pieces were composed in C Major and he thus needed only to add the seven sharps. Several practical editions have transcribed the prelude and fugue into D Flat Major – but are five flats not different from seven sharps?

The Prelude

Forkel has handed down the earliest form of this prelude: it numbered 67 measures which correspond to bars 1–62 and 99–104 of the version in *The Well-Tempered Clavier*. In the *Klavierbüchlein* it is already complete; but it was improved later in several details. The beginning measure (and the corresponding measures 17 and 55) first sounded:

(a version in which the thematic connection with the fugue

[g♯′–e♯″–c♯″] can be heard more clearly than in the later version), also the eighth notes of the transitional measures 8, 16, 24, 54 in the bass were made more flexible.

This prelude, in only two voices, with its wave-like rising and falling figures, a scarcely disguised "*badinerie*," is built entirely in sections of 8 and 4 bars. Only in two places is this regularity broken: measures 31 and 32 are as much the close of the preceding as the beginning of the following phrase, and in bars 87–96 the phrase is extended from 8 to 10 bars – there two measures too few, here two measures too many, so that the total number of bars (104) again is divisible by eight! Moreover, there is a connection with the fugue subject not only at the beginning of the prelude but also in the bass steps f♯–e♯–d♯–c♯ (measures 4–7), which correspond to the lower notes of the broken sixths of the fugue subject. The 4-measure groups of the opening (32 bars) are succeeded by four 4-measure groups (bars 31[1]–46) of which the sequences are derived from bars 7 and 8 of the subject; here the first form of bar 8 (see above) is echoed in the eighth notes a♯″–g♯″–f×″. Now again two 8-measure groups as a reprise on the subdominant, then begins, in the part composed later (from bar 63), a graceful play of frisky little genii (as Schumann might have said), of 12+4+4[2]+4+10 measures. The last eight measures with their brilliant broken harmonies then bring the prelude to a close in high-spirited and self-assured fashion. (Organists will feel themselves reminded of the chords at the end of the F Major toccata (BWV 540), which perhaps may have been conceived at the same time.)

Performance: The last 8 measures show that the prelude should be conceived in virtuoso style, light, nimble, transparent in the 8-measure groups, with verve in the 4-measure groups, *forte* in the last 8 measures. The bass sketches the wave movement along with the theme, and its eighth notes should therefore be slurred forward as well as backward.

[1] A phrase overlap accounts for the duplication of numbers here. – Tr.
[2] Keller omits one 4-measure group here. – Tr.

Couperin wrote in similar circumstances

which is more graphic than one single large bow marking.
Dotted quarter note equals 84 to 92 (i.e., in the tempo of the
fugue).

The Fugue à 3

This fugue is very closely related to its prelude and even exceeds
it in euphony. The subject swings with an elastic turn from
the fifth to the tenth; and then lets itself descend in broken
sixths to the tonic, which it touches only lightly. It surrounds
itself with two regular countersubjects,

of which the first answers the leaping sixth of the subject in
rolling thirds while the second, in legato syncopations gives
stability to the light structure. The rolling thirds we
encounter again in the F Sharp Minor Prelude and in the
A Flat Major Fugue in Book I, the syncopation of the second
countersubject in the (perhaps conceived at the same time)
organ fugue in G Minor (BWV 542). The fugue is made up
of three sections in a special way. The first consists of the
exposition and an incomplete exposition in minor (bass bar
14, alto bar 19) with a close in E Sharp Minor (bar 22). The
middle section similarly has an incomplete exposition (soprano
bar 25 with the upbeat, alto bar 27); then follows a dialogue
between soprano and bass (bars 35–42), which imperceptibly
leads to a recapitulation of the first part, a sort of second exposition, after which a solitary soprano entry (bar 52 with upbeat)
closes the fugue. The concept of the da capo is essentially

foreign to fugue, and yet we find several examples in Bach:
in the C Major unaccompanied Sonata for Violin (BWV 1005)
and in the Organ Fugues in E Minor (BWV 5480) and C Minor
(BWV 537), a demonstration of how little Bach has shut himself
off from the new spirit even in the strict forms of fugue.

The special charm of this fugue lies in the ingenious structure
of the episodes. The first (bar 7) invents a new motive from
a shortened beginning of the subject, which is imitated in the
alto and accompanied in the bass by the thirds of the countersubject:

The close of this motive with its fluttering sixteenths is independently used and imitated in various ways; the leap of a sixth
at the opening is broadened to an octave:

[Keller's example is missing a tie in the middle of the bar. – Tr.]
The tender duet of the two outer voices (bar 35) adds to the
first half of the subject a new countersubject, which falls in
seconds, so that the fugue, as naturally as possible, is filled with
rich thematic life.

For its performance it makes high demands. Usually it is
played too fast and too brilliantly, losing some of its graceful-
ness. The subject might be articulated thus:

If, in bar 2, falling sevenths are heard instead of rising sixths,
the subject is being performed with too much sentimentality.
In bar 7 let the alto part be subordinate to the soprano, in bar
31 the tenor to the bass; the close of the fugue is proud and
self-confident like that of the prelude (the passage work of the

last two bars has the same significance as the last eight bars of the prelude). Quarter note equals 84 to 92 (as in the prelude).

BOOK I: NO. 4 IN C SHARP MINOR, BWV 849

Our idea of the key of C Sharp Minor has been derived very much from Beethoven's so-called "Moonlight Sonata"; Haydn and Mozart gave it little attention. Outside of *The Well-Tempered Clavier*, Bach also used it only rarely, for example in the slow middle movements of his Violin Concerto in E Major (BWV 1042) and the Violin Sonata in the same key (BWV 1016). The special fame of this fugue goes back to the over-enthusiastic judgment of Philipp Spitta, who saw in it "one of the greatest of all creations in the realm of clavier music." If we give it no such exceptional position today, we count it nevertheless, with the fugues in E Flat Minor, F Minor and B Minor, among the most significant in *The Well-Tempered Clavier*. The prelude is the curtain which the fugue, with the entrance of its monumental subject, raises.

The Prelude

Of the eleven preludes whose earlier forms are included in the *Klavierbüchlein für Wilhelm Friedemann Bach*, the three last ones (in C Sharp Minor, E Flat Minor and F Minor) are no longer simple preludes, but arioso movements of great expressiveness. Probably Friedemann, after receiving primarily technical training from the opening numbers, was here to get practice in cantabile playing.

The C Sharp Minor Prelude was taken into *The Well-Tempered Clavier* with few changes; bars 15 and 16 were inserted, and the coda (bars 35–39) tacked on. There are also additional ornaments in Bach's own hand though it is impossible to determine whether they were included from the first or whether – perhaps in teaching – they were added *ad hoc*, as one imagines was the case with certain of the heavily ornamented three-part inventions (e.g., that in F Minor, BWV 795). In a performance on the harpsichord they should be executed in every case.

The prelude is in the style of an invention, although it dispenses with strict voice leading and seems to have been invented at the instrument. As in the two-part invention in C Major (BWV 772), a theme is stated (tonic to dominant), answered with dominant to tonic, spun out thematically, and led by way of sequences to the dominant. Thus far (bar 14), in spite of the caesura in bar 8, it forms one grand melodic line, to whose structure both motives of the theme, (a) and (b), contribute equally. In the second part (from bar 15, with upbeat) the expressive power of the theme is intensified. Bars 15 and 16, which were inserted later and which one can no longer imagine doing without, form an antecedent to bars 17 and 18. From here on the two motives (a) and (b) constantly intermingle; with b♯'' in bar 25, a climax is reached. A broad melodic line seems to lead to a close in bar 35,[1] but Bach, with a deceptive cadence, adds a coda which leads expressively and thematically, directly to the fugue: in bars 35 and 36 the fugue subject appears retrograde in the soprano: c♯''–(e'')–d♯''–e''–b♯'–c♯''[2] (also in the alto in bar 26). This is more convincing than Werker's claim to find the first four notes of the fugue subject in the beginning of the prelude: c♯–b♯ in the bass (bars 1–3), e''–d♯'' in the soprano (bars 3–4).

In performance one should not regard the metric unit as a quarter note, but as a slow dotted half note. Unnecessarily strong accents within each bar are thus avoided, and the *alla breve* movement relates to that of the fugue. One should avoid a too strong *espressivo*: everything that the fugue will have to offer is merely hinted at in the prelude. Dotted half note equals 40.

The Fugue à 5

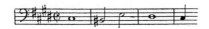

This fugue assumes an exceptional place among the clavier fugues of Bach if only through its display of five voices and three subjects. In both parts of *The Well-Tempered Clavier* only the

[1] Keller: 34. – Tr.   [2] Keller gives the notes in retrograde. – Tr.

B Flat Minor Fugue in Book I is also for five voices. In the organ works of Bach, too, there are only two five-voiced fugues: the one in C Major (BWV 547) and the Triple Fugue in E Flat Major (BWV 552); five-voiced texture was reserved for high church music (the B Minor Mass, BWV 232; *Magnificat*, BWV 243; the Motet, "*Jesu, meine Freude*," BWV 227). Triple fugues are rarer still in Bach's time. But is the C Sharp Minor Fugue a real triple fugue, or merely a fugue with two regular counter-subjects? A quibble with words? No, it strikes at the heart of the matter. One cannot put this fugue on the same level as the two fugues in C Minor and C Sharp Major, which immediately precede it in *The Well-Tempered Clavier*, and whose subjects have two regular countersubjects. In the C Sharp Minor Fugue, the two accompanying subjects may be subordinate to the chief subject and neither of them experiences its own exposition, as in the case of the F Sharp Minor Fugue in Book II, but they have nevertheless such individual traits that one must grant them the status of an individual personality. Each of the three subjects (a, b, c) has its own character. The main subject raises itself laboriously from the tonic over the leading note by way of the painfully dissonant interval of the diminished fourth to the third, and then sinks back to the tonic. One cannot make a greater mistake than to interpret it as a series of two steps of a second, C♯ to B♯ and E to D♯. If one connects the first note by a line with the fourth (C♯ to D♯) and the second with the third (B♯ to E), the figure creates a diagonal, recumbent cross. To Bach himself and his predecessors, this was a well-known symbol: it is found in the *Crucifixus* of a Mass by Johann Kaspar Kerll, and with Bach himself in the crucifixion choruses of the St John and St Matthew Passions (BWV 245, 244). We find ourselves therefore in the most subjective, most sacred area of the art of Bach, without intending to class this fugue as a kind of textless church music. The first countersubject,[1] entering in bar 35 is quite different. It floats without strong individual character from the fifth down to the third and is combined immediately with the first subject. At the same time the move-ment is lightened, the *stylus gravis* of the first part is given up,

---

[1] Keller says "second subject," but to avoid a confusion of this form with sonata form, I have sometimes used the form "first countersubject." Similarly with the "second countersubject," which Keller calls the "third subject." – Tr.

and the number of voices is reduced to three or four. Soon the second countersubject[1] (bar 49), which reaches from the fifth up to the octave and holds firm to it, joins the first two. Reduced to the closest possible position, the three subjects occupy exactly the space of an octave: the chief subject the third from C♯ to E; the first countersubject, the third descending from G♯ back to E, and the second countersubject with the rising fourth from G♯ to C♯.

This fugue divides itself clearly into three sections. In the first, the main subject alone is developed in a vocal five-part movement. In the second (bars 35–94), the two further subjects are added, and combined with the first; in the third section, the first (eighth note) countersubject is eliminated and the chief subject is combined with the second countersubject.

The exposition of the first part piles up the voices from the lowest to the highest, the alto entering irregularly in the subdominant (bar 12); an extra tenor occurs in bar 19. The second exposition, with only four entries of the subject, closes the first section in bar 35 in E major. In the second section, the three themes are combined with one another ten times, four times in the combination a–b–c (bars 49, 54, 59 and 89), twice as a–c–b (bars 66 and 76), three times as b–c–a (bars 68, 74, 81) and once (bar 51) as c–b–a. In the last part of the fugue, the chief subject and the second countersubject clash in such a way that one can only imagine a bitter battle in which the first countersubject by its nature is not equipped to take part. Both subjects redouble their efforts and alternately try to prevail:

[1] See note on previous page.

When the tension of this struggle subsides, the chromatic movement of bars 69–72 is resumed in bar 102. In the last entry of the soprano (bar 107) the third of the subject e″ (bar 109) is syncopated and given the added significance of the sharp dissonance of the diminished seventh, an unprecedented heightening of its expression. In the final cadence we experience, instead of the expected tonic, the cutting dissonance c♯–a–e♯′–g♯′–c♯″, which introduces the final entry of the subject in the alto. That the major close here signifies no liberation, no release of the opposing forces, does not need to be said.

There are still several details of compositional technique to be noticed. In bars 19–25 the subject enters twice in direct succession in the same voice, the second tenor; similarly in bars 25–32, in the first tenor. This voice rests from bars 36–63, and then enters again with the second countersubject. As the second tenor rests only at bar 67, the movement is for a short time (bars 64–66) again five-voiced; in bar 81 the second tenor enters; in bar 82, the first tenor again. In the last bars, the bass must be struck again, because the fugue does not end *pp* as Czerny wished, but with the summoning of full strength.

The performance must clarify the three sections of the fugue, not in the sense of progressive intensification, but so that the first section is performed as if heavily encumbered, the second with a more subjective movement, the final with that highest intensity which is more internal than external. Again here the sign ¢ does not mean a rapid tempo but signifies the older style, especially in the first part. If one takes half note equals 58 to 63 as the tempo, the length of the quarter note is the same as in the prelude.

BOOK I: NO. 5 IN D MAJOR, BWV 850

D major is the traditionally festive tonality of the Baroque, the key of the three trumpets and timpani in the opening chorus of the Christmas Oratorio (BWV 248) and the *Gloria* of the B Minor Mass (BWV 232). The conception of a glittering Baroque display lies at the basis of this fugue as well as of the prelude which leads to it.

The Prelude

In the *Klavierbüchlein für Wilhelm Friedemann Bach* and with Forkel, this prelude appeared in a shorter version of 22 bars which correspond to bars 1–18 and 27–29 of its form in *The Well-Tempered Clavier*. It was indeed conceived as an exacting study for the fingers of the right hand with outstretched thumb and fifth finger, and it fulfils its pedagogical purpose so outstandingly that even today in examinations and contests it is a beloved (and feared) required piece – so little have we gone beyond Bach in two hundred years! Since the left hand only lightly marks the beat, the entire attention can be devoted to the right. Bach expanded it for *The Well-Tempered Clavier* through a recapitulation on the subdominant (bar 20); then the piece abandons its light playful tone, turns toward minor and intensifies – (as in the C Minor Prelude) – to a passionate declamatory close with well-filled-in diminished seventh chords and scale passages, a close through which it seeks and finds a connection to the fugue. This connection is thematically strengthened by the fact that the first three and the last notes of the thirty-second-note figure of the fugue subject are taken from the opening figure of the prelude; the rise to the fifth (d'' to a'') is exceeded in the fugue subject by the sixth d to b.

In three places the extant version is doubtful and contested. On the last quarter note of bar 28 a natural is missing before the f♯''; is the merely an oversight? The manuscript of Schwenke and the editions of Nägeli and Czerny have restored it (compare bar 26); the newer editions have f♯. Equally debatable is the bass in the third-from-last bar. In the autograph there is an A; in Kirnberger, B. I take the B as a subsequent improvement of Bach's: the organpoint is given up, the bass moves via B toward c♯ and to d. Finally: is it intention or carelessness that in the penultimate bar the arpeggio sign is missing on the second quarter beat?

Performance: brisk and graceful (quarter note equals 96), the highest notes lightly separated; in the last third, broadening itself gradually to the tempo of the fugue (quarter note equals 63 to 66).

The Fugue à 4

In no fugue of *The Well-Tempered Clavier* does Bach present himself so openly, is polyphony so subordinated to harmony, as in this one: in none does he stand so near to the style of Handel, especially in the festive orchestral close, which one might ascribe to Handel rather than to Bach. All this derives from the subject. Its haughty bearing, the "defiant shaking of its locks" (Spitta) of the rising thirty-seconds, and the dotted eighths in the style of a French overture fix the character of the fugue. Twice, descending sixteenth notes from on high interpose another force, but this motive is itself derived from the subject through augmentation and inversion. The dissonances, with which the prelude had won its breakthrough to the fugue, are resolved in plain harmony so that in the fugue scarcely a few accidentals are needed. Just as open as its expression is its form. Very little that is technically fugal takes place in it. After the exposition in which the voices enter, as in the C Sharp Minor Fugue, in the order of the lowest to the highest, and after an additional entry in the bass in a low register, an episode of two bars follows (in bar 11) the second and last exposition of the complete subject. From there (bar 17) on, the subject in its entirety does not reappear at all. The episode of bars 9 and 10 is expanded in bars 17–19 to three bars, the thirty-second notes become more and more prolific, and when the performer has mastered the difficulties of bar 24, he is rewarded by the somewhat boastful, not entirely fugue-like close.

In bar 13 the bass entry is debatable. Should the first quarter note be a third higher? Is there an error in Bach's notation? The theme never enters with an octave leap. The free seventh a′ in the alto is suspicious, and the relationship with bar 11 is apparent. That the rhythm ♩♫ is to be understood as ♫♫ has already been dealt with on page 36.

Many interpreters sharpen the punctuation of the eighth notes in the style of the French overture, but surely the coordination of this figure with the 16th notes in bars 9–10 shows that it must be performed as written. Mendelssohn reported in his letters from his travels how he took great care to bring out the subject on the pedals of the organ in Lindau; even as a piece for the fists,[1] it must give many performers difficulty. The author recommends practicing it in the following manner:

Performance: not too stiff or affected, yet with dignity, but also with strength, definition, and a certain fire. Quarter note equals 63 to 66.

BOOK I: NO. 6 IN D MINOR, BWV 851

In Bach's generation the final liberation of the key of D minor from the dorian mode was completed. Bach provided the new tonality with several highly significant works in Weimar and Cöthen: the Organ Toccata (BWV 565), the Partita for Violin Unaccompanied (BWV 1004) and the Chromatic Fantasy and Fugue (BWV 903). We find this same intense feeling in the smaller forms of *The Well-Tempered Clavier*, especially in this fugue, to which the delicate restrained prelude leads in the same way as in Nos. 1 and 4.

[1] The German here is amusing: *auch als "Fauststück" dürfte es manchen Spielern Schwierigkeit bereiten. "Faust"* refers to the old German term, *"Orgel schlagen"* (to "beat" the organ). Because the subject has many 32nd notes, he jokes, it would be difficult even for the "fist" (hand). – Tr.

The Prelude

In a shorter form with only fourteen bars and a concluding bar, this prelude is placed third in the *Klavierbüchlein für Wilhelm Friedemann Bach*, before the D Major Prelude. We can admire again the logical consistency of Bach's teaching of Friedemann: after the first two preludes, which limited themselves to broken chords without a change-of-the-hand position, here a change-of-hand position is required in triplet figuration, although still without passing under the thumb, and indeed only for the right hand, while the left hand keeps time and supports the harmony. For the version in *The Well-Tempered Clavier* Bach, as in preludes and fugues Nos. 2 and 5, has added a second section which shakes it out of its apparent daydreaming. From the climactic "b" (bar 24), chromatic falling triplets in diminished fifths lead to a full-voiced cadence, thence into the fugue. Such chromatic sequences which in the nineteenth century became *clichés* in the hands of Liszt and others, were, in Bach's time, not yet used up and still powerfully expressive. Bach himself, in an early organ prelude in G minor (BWV 535), carried a chain of diminished seventh chords downward through all twelve semitones; he uses the same artistic device with the highest intensity of expression at the close of the Chromatic Fantasy. In the triplet figure of the prelude, a melody is hidden, an "inner voice" as Schumann might have said, which at the beginning could perhaps be indicated: a′–f′–d′–b flat′–g′–e′–c♯′–a′,[1] continuing down to the last note (like the opening of the Brahms Fourth Symphony transposed down a wholetone). The melodic voices support each other so that in bar 10 one seems to hear a four-voiced movement:

This alone should prevent the prelude from being played too lightly and too casually. The triplets are naturally anacrustic

---

[1] Keller here says "c♯′–f′," an obvious misprint. – Tr.

throughout, but one should be very sparing with caesuras. These are indicated chiefly by the use of larger intervals in the bass part, e.g., in bars 10 and 11 there should be a separation before the second and sixth eighth notes; but this should be avoided in bars 12–14. Whether in bars 16 and 17 the second half should be played in the manner of an echo may be left to the judgment of the player. Toward the close the movement is broadened so that the eighth note becomes like the quarter note of the fugue. Quarter note equals 52 decreasing to 36.

The Fugue à 3

The counterpoint of this fugue is among the strictest in *The Well-Tempered Clavier*. It eschews no dissonance and places so small a value upon euphony that one can understand if players do not particularly like it. But how much it has to give him who is not afraid of its thorns! The subject rises from the tonic with a measured step, then with a soaring leap to the sixth, breaks off and turns back to the fifth. It is significant that on this sixth, b flat', a staccato sign appears – the only autograph one in the first volume of *The Well-Tempered Clavier*; it is also significant that Bach, contrary to his usual custom, carries the staccato signs through the entire fugue (they appear even in the sequences of bars 9–11). This shows that he conceived the subject as violent, aggressive. The continuation of the subject, which serves as a connection with the countersubject:

is, when reversed, like the beginning of the subject (e–g–f–e–d backwards equals d–e–f–g–e). The regular countersubject

also derives from the subject, but it loses something of its significance through the early entries of the stretto. In precision, the two-part form of this fugue is surpassed only by that of the E Minor Fugue. Both parts (bars 1–21 and 21–42, to which there are two bars of cadential extension) are not only precisely of the same length but of equal construction. The four closing bars of each half (bars 17–20 in A minor and bars 39–42 in D minor) are exactly alike. There are many more formal correspondences. Bars 6 and 7 (subject in the bass) have their correspondence in bars 27 and 28 (subject in the soprano in inversion); likewise, bars 8 and 9 (subject in the soprano) in bars 29 and 30 (subject in the inversion in the bass); the veiled subject entry in the bass (bar 11)

enters in the soprano in bar 32; the double-entry of the alto and bass simultaneously (alto inverted) in bar 14 returns in bar 35 (soprano and alto). There are stretti of many kinds: at the octave at one measure distance (bars 17–18 and 39–40), at the lower fifth and inverted in the imitating voice, bars 13 (soprano) and 14 (alto); between the soprano in inversion and alto (bars 27–28), and in the alto with the bass in inversion at the fourth below (bars 28–29); between the bass and the soprano in inversion (bars 21–22); and between this voice and the bass also in inversion at the seventh (!) in bars 22–23, not to mention incomplete entries. It does not need saying that all these devices are used not for their own sake but to strengthen the power inherent in the subject; we see a confrontation of the artist with his material in the smallest of space and with the most sparing means. As the trill in the subject after the staccato on B flat enters freely, it can begin with the main note, as can the trills of the entering turn in bars 9–11.[1] In bars 15, 16, 28 and 29 the trill signs should be supplied. The eighth notes of the subject require an accentuated legato; after f' in bar 2, a small caesura should be introduced. The tempo is a controlled *allegro marcato*. Quarter note equals 72.

[1] In the *Revisionsbericht* to his edition, Kreutz points out that the Bach autograph has no signs in bars 9–11; Anna Magdalena's copy has "tr" indicated here. A copy made from Anna Magdalena's copy indicates a *pralltrill*. One wonders why Kreutz used the turn, which is only confusing, instead of the *tr* or *pralltrill*. – Tr.

BOOK I: NO. 7 IN E FLAT MAJOR, BWV 852

Bach rarely used the key of E Flat Major, a favorite of the Viennese classics, in his Weimar and Cöthen periods. E Flat Major is also missing in the *Klavierbüchlein für Wilhelm Friedemann Bach*, which includes all the other keys, and this is probably why Bach here had to go back to an earlier work. The composition which he chose for that purpose looks very strange indeed in *The Well-Tempered Clavier*, for the alleged prelude is in reality a preamble with a double fugue; thus, it stands in no relationship whatever to the graceful fugue which follows it in *The Well-Tempered Clavier*. What could have induced him to put it into this place, where through its size and style it seems to be an interloper? It would seem that he wanted to preserve a work from his youth that had special significance for him, and for which *The Well-Tempered Clavier* seemed a good home. It will be well to consider this prelude and the fugue independently of each other.

The Prelude

In the seventeenth century the name *präludium* was often given to a prelude with a fugue attached to it, in much the same way as Bach's orchestral suites are called simply "Overtures." Only in that sense can this prelude justify its title, for it is a preamble with a spaciously developed double fugue.

Its structure is as follows: preamble, bars 1–9; fugato in the older style, bars 10–24; connecting to a fugue with two paired subjects: a somewhat more developed version of the fugato subject and the 16th-note motive of the preamble (bars 25–70) combined like this:

The exposition closes in bar 35 in G minor; the second exposition intensifies in technique through a stretto of the first subject (soprano and alto bar 35, soprano and tenor bars 38–39, alto and tenor bars 41–42, bass and tenor bars 46–47). The third exposition begins in the middle of bar 49 (first subject in the bass, second subject in the alto). The stretti subside; in bars 57^1–62 the fugue reaches a climax which Bach no doubt recalled when writing the last part of his Triple Fugue for Organ.

Here the fugue has reached a spiritual peak which it maintains to the close. First the soprano and alto unite once again in a chain of stretti of the first subject,

then the fugue dies away over a tonic organpoint with one last entrance of both themes in grand style.

While giving all admiration to this remarkable work we must not overlook some signs of immaturity: the unmotivated doubling of the speed in bar 8 (which the performer must make credible through a retardation); the displacement of the metric accent of the subject in the soprano bars 12–13 (a typical trademark of the older style); the leading of the soprano in bar 43 below the tenor, a position from which only a daring leap can save it; but above all its closely knit texture, which stays almost entirely in the middle register up to bar 57; and its length, which it has in common with a series of other youthful fugues of Bach: the concluding fugue of the toccatas in D minor, E minor, C minor and G major, the B Minor Fugue on the subject of Albinoni, and others. All these fugues give an impression of length, because their form is not sufficiently taut, while the fugue to the Chromatic Fantasy (BWV 903), though longer in number of bars, does not seem long to the listener.

With rare discernment, Busoni regarded three of Bach's E flat major subjects as related to one another: this one, the subject of the fugue in Book II of *The Well-Tempered Clavier*, and in a

[1] Keller: 58. – Tr.

sense of progressive intensification, climaxing in the Organ
Fugue. He also suggested exchanging the E Flat Major Preludes
in Book I and Book II – this would especially benefit the fugue
in Book I – but dare we separate what Bach has put together?

The performance should be quiet, collected, with the objec-
tivity of organ sound, the tempo measured, but not dragging.
Quarter note equals 60.

The Fugue à 3

This fugue, one of the most charming in *The Well-Tempered
Clavier*, runs the danger of being overwhelmed by its Prelude;
it should therefore be considered without relationship to it.
Together with the fugues in C Minor, F Sharp Major and
G Sharp Minor it is one of the freest, most modern fugues in
The Well-Tempered Clavier. It is the first clavier fugue of Bach
whose subject modulates to the dominant. With the exception
of a youthful fugue in E Minor (BWV 945), whose subject
modulates to the subdominant (!), and the fugue to the Organ
Toccata in C Major (BWV 566), all of his previous fugue subjects
had remained in the tonic. The eighth rest in the course of the
subject makes it easy for the *comes* to find its way back. The
subject hovers pleasantly on the fifth, the tonic note is only
lightly touched, the break after the two eighth notes has a
capricious effect. But how firmly it is joined together: the upbeat of the two 16th notes after the rest is an abbreviation of
the 16th notes in the first bar, the two eighth notes e flat″–d″
bear a relationship to the eighth notes c″–b flat′; the fluttering
appendix to the subject supplies the material for the episode.
The countersubject too is closely related to the subject:

Thus from a, b and c a fugue is built of which Werker says,
"it is from the first to the last note a masterpiece of great beauty,

which has neither a topheavy nor a bottomheavy theme, only balance." It is in two sections. In the first section (bars 1–17) there is only a single entrance in the soprano (bar 11) after the exposition. The second section (bars 17–37) contains two expositions: one of only the alto and bass in the minor (bars 17 and 20), and a complete one in the order of bass (bar 26), soprano (bar 29) and alto (bar 34). Since all entries are separated by shorter or longer episodes, one can scarcely speak of completed expositions, but rather of individual entrances which are connected to each another through episodes. These are not carried by figure (c) alone, but also by the little upbeat motive which entered in the soprano as early as bars 3–4 and in bars 7–9 was broadened to eighth notes. Similarly the three upbeat eighth notes of the alto in bars 7–9 are taken from (c) through augmentation. At the conclusion of each section there is chromaticism; in bars 15–17 with a falling sequence built on figure (c), which was outlined in bar 5, and in the startlingly dissonant cut-off in bar 34, which however is to be conceived as playful.

Performance: the eighth notes c''–b flat' in the subject should be separated sharply, the eighth notes e flat''–d'' more gently. The trill begins on the main note, in order to avoid the repetition of a note. The first of the four sixteenth notes should be lightly detached especially in figure (c). The trill must be played out; it should be completed in bars 27 and 35 as a *pralltrill*;[1] in bars 7 and 21 a *pralltrill* is also sufficient. The tempo should be gently moving, not hurried or too rushed. Quarter note equals 84 to 92.

BOOK I: NO. 8 IN E FLAT MINOR, D SHARP MINOR, BWV 853

How did it happen that Bach put together a prelude in E flat minor with a fugue in D sharp minor? Why not both in E flat minor or both in D sharp minor? Spitta gave the obvious

---

[1] When Keller here says *"Praller,"* a conventional translation of the word might well be "inverted mordent." I have preferred to translate this as *pralltrill*, in order to call attention to the fact that this is not the inverted mordent of the Romantic period, which precedes the beat, but that it occurs generally on the beat and is not limited to one alternation of notes. – Tr.

answer; the fugue was originally in D minor, and Bach needed only – as in the case of the C Sharp Major Prelude and Fugue – to alter the signature, thereby sparing himself the trouble of having to copy out the fugue again. The prelude was already composed (it was in the *Klavierbüchlein für Wilhelm Friedemann Bach*), though in E flat minor, but Bach took the discrepancy of the keys, which seems disturbing to us, in his stride. Spitta was confirmed in his supposition by the rising scale of the soprano in bar 15 of the fugue, which must be bent rather crudely in order not to exceed the range c''':

In D minor it can be led up to the octave:

and the player should have no scruples about making this alteration, which represents Bach's original intention. Most practical editions have rightly transposed the fugue to E flat minor, because the difference of the keys almost destroys the unity of prelude and fugue, which Bach sacrificed only for the practical reason I have given above. Thus the "D Sharp Minor Fugue" will not be discussed here, but rather the "E Flat Minor Fugue."

The Prelude

Mattheson acknowledged that he had never seen a piece in E flat minor, and even with Bach this key occurs in only one other place, the second minuet of the Fourth French Suite (BWV 815). The strangeness of the key gives the prelude an uncommon magic; the effect is strengthened through the solemn 3/2 meter and through the harp-like chords over which a duet of two mutually answering voices rises. The result is unique for its time – the first nocturne in clavier music, a nocturne with the clarity of a starry night. When, in the middle of the prelude, the two solo voices intertwine (bars 20–23), the broken chords sound on inaudibly. In its earliest form, which Forkel passed on, the coda of bars 29–36 is still missing; the half cadence in B flat minor lay exactly in the middle, the declamatory rise of bars 25–28 was the climactic close. In *The Well-Tempered Clavier*, however, a deceptive cadence in bar 29 leads to a second climax, given first to the bass, then transferred to the soprano, which rises high before it falls to the cadence (an octave lower than bar 28). Yet this is not the end; only after three further measures does the movement come entirely to rest.

The arpeggio signs are missing in the first three and the last three bars; the harmonies thus should only gradually be set in motion, and similarly again be brought to rest. In the copy of Anna Magdalena there are slurs in bar 20,

in order that an upbeat performance (which seems possible) should be avoided. The bold passage e flat''–d flat''–c'' in bars 10–11 has been attenuated in many manuscripts and editions, but it is authentic and truly Bach-like.

The chords should be broken solemnly, the melodic voices should be expressive but not tender or sentimental; they must couple gentleness with nobility. The metric units are the half notes. Half note equals 44.

The Fugue à 3

This fugue is one of the most important in *The Well-Tempered Clavier*; but would we attach the same significance to it if it had been handed down individually as "Fugue in D Minor"? Scarcely. We would have then included it in the list of Bach's youthful fugues, which we were discussing in connection with the E Flat Major Prelude, and we would include that Prelude, together with this and the A Minor Fugue among those works which were not originally intended for *The Well-Tempered Clavier.* But now it has its place in the collection and it has an inseparable bond with its independently conceived prelude. After the meditative prelude we are led, pensively, to a higher level with a broader, greater horizon; it is as though the eye, no longer daydreaming, but searching, is raised to heaven. This spiritual intensity lets us forget the fugue's rhythmic monotony; it is by way of the spiritual intensification of the counterpoint that we are led to still greater heights than in the prelude.

A fugue subject on which so many techniques are used must have special characteristics. The subject of the E Flat Minor Fugue is such a one. It is constructed from two half arches which collide in the middle (on e flat'), one large precipitously rising, then gently falling, arch. That the two ascents e flat' to b flat' and e flat' to a flat' are not anacrustic, but on accented parts of the bar give the subject an indecisive quality, a vacillating balance. In scarcely any other fugue does one feel the accent of the bar so little as here. A countersubject with strong profile is missing in order that the subject may be counterpointed continually with itself; also, the few episodes serve only as transitions. Thus this fugue is carried by the subject alone; its transparent structure facilitates attention to the middle voice, its leading of line avoids any harshness.

The plan of the fugue is as follows:

1. Exposition: bars 1–19 (E flat minor to B flat minor).
2. Exposition: stretto of the subject (B flat minor–G flat major), bars 19–29.
3. Exposition: subject in inversion (G flat major–E flat minor), bars 30–44.
4. Exposition: stretto in inversion, bars 44–52.
5. Exposition: two threefold stretti, bars 52–61.
6. Exposition: subject in augmentation, with stretti of all sorts (bars 62–87).

One recognizes at first glance the well-conceived growth from the first to the last exposition. Since the fourth and the fifth hang closely together, they could also be regarded as one continuous exposition.

As in many other fugues, Bach here prolongs the exposition

by permitting the third voice to enter first (bar 8) in the position of the tenor as *dux*, then once again (bar 12) as *comes* in the position of the bass, as though the fugue were four-voiced.

The stretto in the second exposition occurs between the alto and soprano at a half measure's distance at the octave (bars 19–20); then in all three voices (with certain freedoms) from bar 24, with the alto augmented and dotted; bar 27 adds a second stretto by the soprano and the alto at the lower fifth. In the third exposition, the subject is turned toward major and inverted; the soprano enters in bar 30, the alto in bar 36, the brass in a high position, almost a tenor, in bar 39. The beginning of the second half of the fugue is clarified through rests in the bass (they are almost the only ones in the entire fugue!); beginning in a low position with the inversion of the subject, the soprano (intertwined with the alto) follows two quarters later. The fourth exposition corresponds to the first, as a comparison of bars 47–50 with bars 24–27 shows: the subject in dotted rhythm here appears in the soprano, the normal form in the alto, the bass leads more freely. In the fifth exposition the three voices enter in a stretto at a distance of a quarter note, first in the normal then in the inverted position. The stretto goes by so quickly that the listener scarcely has time to take it in:

Then the soprano swings on high with the extended subject,

sinks slowly down, and thus prepares the final exposition which surpasses all that has gone before: the subject enters in notes of double value and has as counterpoints the subject in its normal values in regular as well as in inverted movement (in the following sketch the non-thematic voices are omitted):

These almost incredible combinations of the subject are naturally much more than a mere expression of a very highly developed contrapuntal technique. The augmentation of a subject is for Bach a symbol of inner greatness, as for example in the first *Credo* and in the *Confiteor* of the B Minor Mass (BWV 232), in the opening choruses of the Cantatas BWV 80 ("*Ein feste Burg ist unser Gott*") and 77 ("*Du sollst Gott, deinen Herren, lieben,*" on "*Dies sind die heil'gen zehn Gebot*") and at the close of the Organ Fugue in C Major (BWV 547). From this, the final exposition of the fugue gains a breadth and solemnity which one could not have guessed at its beginning. One almost regrets that the soprano with its two other voices must descend in bar 81 to lift itself again, almost laboriously, to the final cadence.

The performer who wishes to emphasize this evolution may give less attention to the individual entries of the subject than to the setting-off of the six (or five) expositions as complete units from one another, perhaps in the dynamic shading *mp*, *mf*, *p*, *mf*, *f*, in which the last *forte* may be more inwardly felt than superficially accented. In the subject itself a light separation of e flat′ and a flat′ is appropriate to the syncopation of the a flat′ without this note's having to be accented. The tempo is neither dragging nor fluent, but flowing gently, perhaps one and a half times that of the Prelude. Quarter note equals 60 to 66.

Before the introduction of equal temperament, E major, because of the notes G sharp and D sharp, was a feared and rarely used tonality; Bach used it already in a modern sense, as the Sixth French Suite (BWV 817) shows. In one copy of the French Suites, this prelude was placed at the beginning of No. 6; from the point of view of its mood, it would have fitted there exceptionally well; but in the final editing Bach left all of the French Suites without preludes.

The Prelude

This prelude seems simple, but has a happy euphony and a formal balance. It is a *pastorale* (the only one in the first volume of *The Well-Tempered Clavier*) in the traditional 12/8 rhythm, the meter of the pastoral compositions of the Italians as well as the shepherds' music in *The Messiah* and in the *Christmas Oratorio* (BWV 248). It has a three-part song form, like a little early classic sonata movement: exposition from bar 1 to the middle of bar 8, middle section (like a little development) from middle of bar 8–14, recapitulation in the sub-dominant, from bars 15–24. This movement is three-voiced, although for technical reasons, the middle voice drops out in certain places: in bar 4, there is missing an f sharp';[1] bar 9, d sharp'; bar 17, e'; bar 18, b. The chromaticism with which the cadence is prepared at the close of the first and third parts is so exquisite that one can understand (if indeed with reservations) that Gray felt reminded by it of Chopin and Bellini. Riemann described the prelude with poetic rapture: "Like boughs clad with new foliage the light arpeggio triplets sway, with their motion at the tips of the branches, as though rippled by the wind with cheerful little trills of the feathered songsters sheltered within; below reigns peace (a resting bass and a slowly accompanying

[1] Keller: f sharp". – Tr.

middle voice) . . ." – and yet people say that Riemann was a dry theorist!

Performance: moving gracefully, not hurried. Dotted quarter note equals 63 to 69.

The Fugue à 3

This fugue, which has no recognizable thematic connection with the prelude, substitutes strength and movement for the former's quiet grace. Brandt-Buys calls it "happily radiant, self-confident, high-spirited and untroubled by hidden depths." Its cheeky subject, rising and then continuing in streaming movement, leads into the countersubject without a clear break. According to Czackes, the subject ends with the first note of the second bar (?), a melancholy torso; in the middle of this bar one still feels no close, but there is a stronger impression that the subject ends at the beginning of the third bar, thus putting it in the category of those which modulate to the dominant, and which – like the theme of the A Major Fugue – enter immediately in stretto – a state of affairs, remarkably enough, that seems not to have been observed before. Hence, the *comes* then modulates back again, and the third voice leads as *dux* again to the dominant. A second exposition in which the soprano leads to a higher register follows the first exposition unusually closely. The form of this fugue can be regarded as two-part in a special manner: two halves (bars 1–12 and 17–29) lie on either side of a four-barred middle section in C Sharp Minor (bars 13–16), which is introduced through a varied entry in the soprano

and closed with a single tenor entry. Now follows a re-exposition, again in major, in all three voices, beginning with the bass (bar 19), which the soprano, with lengthened upbeat, follows in bar 20, the alto in bar 21. In the last re-exposition the victoriously entering soprano is deflected and lengthened; the alto and bass (bars 27–28) also want to enter the conversation, but their speech is abruptly cut off, and Bach closes the fugue masterfully and self-confidently (after upsetting respectable people through parallel fourths on the third quarter of the penultimate bar). How much caprice and high spirit, but also what painful care in the purity of the structure is evident in this fugue! Bach subsequently altered the leading of the bass in bars 24–27, in order to eliminate parallel diminished and pure fifths which were created through the stepwise eighth notes of the bass. In the process he abandoned the scalewise movement of the bass

in favor of a jagged line

in which one can see a relationship to the opening notes of the subject. (From a purely musical point of view the first conception was perhaps the better one, as the fifths were hardly noticed by the ear.)

Performance: with energy and fire, but not in the hurried tempo in which the fugue is so often played. Quarter note equals 96 to 104.

BOOK I: NO. 10 IN E MINOR, BWV 855

Bach conceived the key of E minor as masculine and powerful, a quite different conception from that of the Viennese classical and romantic composers (e.g., Mendelssohn, music for *A Midsummer Night's Dream* and the Violin Concerto). Bach's concept of E minor is to be observed in the great Organ Prelude and Fugue (BWV 548) as well as in the two fugues in *The Well-Tempered Clavier* and the second half of the prelude in Book I.

The Prelude

Of all the preludes which Bach took over from the *Klavierbüchlein
für Wilhelm Friedemann Bach* into *The Well-Tempered Clavier*, this
one was the most thoroughly rewritten. In its earlier form it
numbered only 23 bars, and the bass moved in sixteenth notes
(giving Friedemann's left-hand practice in evenness of touch);
the right hand was confined to short, continuo chords, in order
that the left could claim all his attention.

Since in this form (BWV 855a) it was too short and musically
inadequate for *The Well-Tempered Clavier*, Bach superimposed
an ornamented melody on the harmonic model and added a
second section to it, marked "*presto*," in which, now at doubled
tempo, both hands had to perform the figuration of the first
section. If one should think of the first part as orchestrated (the
ornamented melody with a flute or oboe, the chord-like accompaniment with a lute, the bass with a cello), the second part is
unquestionably clavier music. This creates a danger that the
prelude may fall apart in performance if the transfer from one
section to the other is made abruptly without preparation. If the
presto is reached by way of a *stringendo* in the closing bars of the
opening section to exactly the doubled tempo, the unity of the
prelude can be preserved. The somewhat affected, sentimental
character of the melody is particularly clear in the tender
"suspension," the rest before the mordent after the trills in bars
10 and 12, a piece of writing characteristic of the French
clavecinists which Bach employs in only one other place, the
French Overture (BWV 831). In this prelude, too, we find Bach
intent on utmost purity of texture: in bars 9 and 15 he crosses
the middle voices in order to avoid octaves with the bass on

corresponding beats.[1] As in Nos 2, 5 and 6 the second part of the prelude supplies a direct connection with the fugue.

Performance: in the first part, the melody delicately expressive, the chords *pp*, the bass *p*; in the second, everything *forte*. Tempo of the first part, quarter note equals 58 to 63; of the second, quarter note equals 116 to 126.

The Fugue à 2

This fugue is the only one for two voices which Bach wrote, if one ignores a fughetta of doubtful authenticity in C Minor (BWV 961).[2] It stems directly from the prelude and surpasses it in its aggressive quality. The subject with its hidden two-voicedness and descending chromaticism has a precedent in the subject of the concluding fugue of the Toccata in E Minor (BWV 914) and a successor in the great Organ Fugue (BWV 548) in the same key. It modulates to the dominant; has a real answer; but (uniquely in Bach) it does not modulate back again, but goes on to the second dominant.[3] If the subject and its answer are already willful, the structure of the fugue is even more so. It consists of two halves of precisely the same length and the same structure (bars 1–19 and 20–39), to which a four-bar coda is appended. The second part is like the first but with an exchange of the voices and a small deviation in bar 29 in order to effect the return to E minor. Each part has two expositions: in the first part the second exposition is in major (soprano bar 11, bass bar 13); in the second, in minor (bass bar 30, soprano bar 32), so that the close in E minor is reached from the subdominant. The coda contains the beginning of a stretto

[1] Note: this voice leading is not preserved in the *Bach Gesellschaft* Volume 15, page 38. – Tr.

[2] The two-voiced fugue contained in the prelude of the C Minor Partita is not a complete and separate work. – Tr.

[3] Technically this is not quite correct. Bach moves not to F♯ minor, but to the dominant of B minor. Thus the bass at the beginning of bar 5 takes A♯ rather than A. But the modulation certainly does not return to the expected E minor. – Tr.

which would be real if the bass in bar 40 imitated the soprano exactly. Bach, however, deviated on the grounds of textural purity (in order to avoid parallel diminished and pure fifths). In a two-voiced fugue, the episodes play a large role. The first (bars 5–10 in the first section; bars 24–29 in the second) develops sequences from the material of the opening; the second (bars 15–19 and correspondingly 34–38) augments the broken triad of the subject to eighth notes and places them against an off-beat scalewise motive taken from the countersubject (bar 3) which in its downward movement traverses the sixth with which the subject ends. If such a fugue as this wishes to reduce the number of its voices, it can only become monodic. The unison of bars 19 and 38 is an example of this uncommon occurrence; it is effective here not as a relaxation of tension, but rather as a gathering of forces before the beginning of the second part and before the coda, which lets the subject disappear as if from the earth in an abrupt close.

Performance: lively and passionate, richly colored, in the tempo of the second half of the prelude. Quarter note equals 116 to 126.

BOOK I: NO. 11 IN F MAJOR, BWV 856

Like C major, F major is a neutral key, a favorite in the Viennese classic period for *andante* movements; with Bach quite frequently in small forms (inventions, little preludes) it expresses "a contented spirit which takes delight in good order" (Mattheson).

The Prelude

This prelude was taken over without alteration from the *Klavierbüchlein für Wilhelm Friedemann Bach*, excepting the addition of turns to the trills. It is an outstanding study in finger playing, in which the weaker fingers of the outstretched hand are employed while the passing under of the thumb still is avoided wherever possible. If it is played as fast and as nimbly as required, then the coincidence of the capricious trills with the sixteenth notes of the other hand will give many performers something to worry about. How indeed may the young Friedemann have coped with it? From the point of view of technique of composition, this prelude is a two-part invention whose double subject (the eighth notes of the bass are also thematic) is developed in the usual manner: the motive is divided into half measures between the two voices and spun out in sequences (bars 3 to the middle of 6); then the play repeats itself with exchanged voices (to the middle of bar 12), the trills are extended into chains, the driving motive lifts itself from the lowest to the highest position and falls, whirling, into a short broken-off cadence. Such cadences, for the most part intended to be high-spirited, are found especially in Bach's youthful works, e.g., the fugue to the Organ Toccata in C Major (bwv 564), the Organ Fugue in D Major (bwv 532), the Toccatas in C Minor and G Major (bwv 911 and 916). The trills begin with a turn from below, except at the beginning of bars 4 and 9 when they begin from above probably in order to avoid the chromatic leading b flat' to b' and f'' to f sharp''. This also serves to maintain the purity of the texture. In bar 7, Kirnberger's manuscript has E in the bass (in the place of D) on the last quarter, a striking coincidence with the same alteration in bar 33 of the D Major Prelude, and, as in that instance, an improvement.

This prelude sounds splendid on the harpsichord; on the piano, only with a light tonal quality, virtuoso performance of the trills, and in lively tempo. Dotted quarter note equals 76 to 84.

The Fugue à 3

This fugue has the rhythm and deliberate grace of a *passepied* in the manner of the last fugue in Book II, but is the more strictly worked out of the two. Its four-bar subject goes back to one of J. K. F. Fischer (from the *Ariadne Musica*):

But how much more flowing and subtle it has become with Bach! As in the fugue subjects in C Major and E Major, its end flows imperceptibly into the countersubject. Not only its four-measure groups, but also its two-part form, gives the fugue the character of a dance movement. It consists of two sections of exactly equal length – 36 bars each, and these 72 3/8 bars taken together are exactly as long as the 18 12/8 bars of the prelude. Each of the two halves consists of two complete expositions (bars 1–17 and 18–29 in the first part, bars 36–46 and 47–56 in the second) and an additional alto entry (bar 28 with an upbeat in the first part), which in the second section, transformed and lengthened, closes the fugue:

Within the second part, bars 36–46 (D minor) and 46–56 (G minor) correspond exactly with one another. In the last section of the fugue (from bar 56) Bach introduces a rising scale, derived by inversion from the first bar of the fugue subject, which transfers to the soprano in bar 60 and is combined with this motive

taken from bar 3. The stretti of the subject in bars 36–38 and 46–48 had implied an increased intensity as compared with the first part; now however the fugue displays a size and breadth not foreshadowed earlier. Forkel does this fugue an injustice when he numbers it among those in *The Well-Tempered Clavier* "which one can accuse of containing imperfections" (the others are for him: C Major [!], F Minor [!], G Major [!], G Minor and A Minor).

Performance: since Czerny, it has become customary to slur

the upbeat and to separate the three following eighth notes; this lends wings, as it were, to the subject, but it does not conform to Baroque usage. Dotted quarter note equals 50 to 54.

BOOK I: NO. 12 IN F MINOR, BWV 857

We are now halfway through the cycle of the keys, and take a backward glance before continuing our journey. With one exception, all the preludes in the first half were already extant, though there are no earlier forms or preliminary sketches for the fugues. The remaining preludes as well as fugues had to be newly composed. We could see in the first half of Book I how the preludes were first worked out as scale passages and broken chords, and later increasingly endowed with individual character, a development that can be followed from their arrangement in *Klavierbüchlein für Wilhelm Friedemann Bach* rather than from the order in which they stand in *The Well-Tempered Clavier*. In the second half there are only two toccata-like preludes: those in G Major and B Flat Major. All the others are clearly related to their fugue, even if they are not dependent on them. Thus at No. 12, we have actually arrived at a caesura. Bach himself emphasized it by giving this fugue a most unusual chromatic subject, which can be compared only with the last fugue (No. 24). The two have in common their structure as well as the contrast of their diatonic episodes with the chromatic subject.

With Bach the key of F minor often expresses a deep seriousness, of which the introductory chorus of the Cantata, BWV 12 (*"Weinen, Klagen, Sorgen, Zagen"*), is an example.

The Prelude

In the preface to his edition of *The Well-Tempered Clavier* Czerny has expressed the opinion that these preludes and fugues can be played equally well on the piano or the organ. The only prelude in Book I in which this proves to be true is that in F Minor, an example of the legato style whose texture is relaxed by scarcely even a rest. It is not truly four-voiced like an organ piece, but becomes four-voiced only through the sustaining of the quarter notes, which are meant to make the rapidly fading sound of a stringed keyboard instrument sound fuller. Since the subject consists of broken chords, changing notes and passing tones, from the point of view of writing technique, harmonic and contrapuntal style are here mingled together. We know its shorter, original version through a manuscript of Forkel, in which it closes after bar 15 with these two measures:

(The complete form already exists in the *Klavierbüchlein.*) In the Forkel version, the half cadence on A flat major (bar 9) lies exactly in the middle: in the *Klavierbüchlein* and *The Well-Tempered Clavier* there is a change from the middle of bar 16, as in the preludes in C Minor, D Major and D Minor, to a broadening of the melodic lines and an intensification of the expression which prepare for the grandeur of the fugue. In this coda, rising high and again falling, the subject of the fugue is already recognizable, shadow-like, in gigantic augmentation:

Performance: strictly legato with the steadiness and repose of organ tone; in slow tempo. Quarter note equals 48 to 56.

The Fugue à 4

This fugue, which further deepens the earnestness of the prelude, is spiritually one of the most significant in *The Well-Tempered Clavier.* Its almost purely chromatic subject is unique in the collection. In slow, measured quarter-note movement it circumscribes the fifth and lifts itself with the apparently consonant fourth b to e′ (which here has the effect of a cutting dissonance) to the octave. It now drops a fifth (note here again the chromatic connections from f′ and b flat to b and e′)[1] and sinks slowly first chromatically, then diatonically to the tonic note. The powers, confined and even banned in the anguished line of the subject, which rears up and then sinks back exhausted, are unchained and set free in the two regular countersubjects. The first

makes four powerful assaults against the subject and reaches the octave as its goal. The second countersubject

strengthens the first, but is subordinated to it. The three subjects together create a texture of uncommon harshness and dissonance. Opposed against this complex are appeasing, purely diatonic episodes which do not have the task of connecting the entrances of the subject, but form a conscious contrast with it. They are taken from the short transitional motive in bar 4, a rhythmic figure much used by Bach in his cantatas, which Schweitzer has described as the "joy" motive. Here, however, it must be regarded more generally as an expression of quiet, inner harmony:

To enhance this mood, Bach here rejects closed expositions so completely that he even interrupts the first exposition itself with an episode (bars 10–14) inserted between the entries of the bass and soprano; both enter, contrary to the rules, as *dux*. From this point on there is no re-exposition of more than two voices: of tenor and bass in bars 19 and 27 (and these are widely separated from one another), alto and tenor in bars 34 and 40 in major

[1] Keller means here to call attention to the relationship of the E moving to F chromatically and the chromatic fall of B natural to B flat. – Tr.

(in which version the subject forfeits something of its expressive power), and finally soprano and bass in the highest position of the soprano and the lowest of the bass, in bars 47 and 53. The particular form of this fugue (which we will meet again in the B Minor Fugue) is better and more correctly grasped by our rejecting the concept of a regular closed exposition and concentrating on its main principle, the alternation of the chromatic subject and the diatonic episodes. It then appears to have the qualities of a rondo (in the sense of a rondo in the old French style) in which we must admire the varied ways in which Bach has managed the interludes between the entries of the main theme; they are as alike as the pillars of a Gothic cathedral and yet, like them, all differ from one another. The episodes are only three-voiced, leaving free the space for the voice in which the subject will enter. Only the penultimate episode (bars 43–47) is four-voiced, but at its end the soprano sinks so low that its entry on g'' is felt as a new voice. The fugue has no final climax; a spell is cast at the beginning from which there is no release until the end. The absence of the usual trill on the penultimate note of the subject (in the fugues in F Sharp Minor, B Major and B Minor it at least still appears at the beginning), and the specific absence of all ornamentation is also a sign of the deep seriousness with which it is pervaded.

The performance must carefully underline the contrast between the thematic parts and the episodes (the contrast of the "dual principal," as Beethoven might have said). Quarter note equals 48 to 56 (as in the prelude).

BOOK I: NO. 13 IN F SHARP MAJOR, BWV 858

After the dark, heavy pathos of the F Minor Fugue, we are here surrounded by the delicacy and muted light of the key with the largest number of sharps in common use. The romantics (Chopin, Schumann) conceived it as full of feeling, Beethoven in his Sonata Opus 78 made it playful, Mozart avoided it entirely, Haydn used it in his Quartet Opus 76 No. 5, Hoboken III: 79 ("*Largo cantabile e mesto*"), with the expression of mournful solemnity, Scarlatti made it elegant in his two F Sharp Major Sonatas; but no one has captured its fragrance as has Bach.

The Prelude

The special charm of this prelude lies not only in its key, but also in the delicacy of its transparent two-voiced texture and the meter chosen, the 12/16 rhythm, as one might say a duo-decimal version of the 12/8 measure. The prelude has a form peculiar to itself: six similar sections which run through the tonal circle of F sharp major–C sharp major–D sharp minor–A sharp minor–G sharp minor–F sharp major; three sections in major, three in minor (bar 1 to the middle of 6, to 12, to the middle of 15, to the middle of 18, to the middle of 24, to 30). In the two middle sections the six-bar phrases are shortened to three bars. Every section begins with the broken triad motive which is taken up by the opposite voice and developed in inter-locked rhythm. The final section turns surprisingly toward minor, but in the next-to-last bar the major triad with its total "sweetness" enters again the highest position of the soprano. In bars 5, 14, 17 and 28 in many editions there are incorrect slurs in the soprano between the third and fourth eighth notes. In the autograph copy there are trill signs only in bars 7, 12 (twice), 13 and 19; it is up to the performer to insert them in bars 1 and 16.

Performance: the ideal instrument is the clavichord with its delicate tonal quality, capable of the finest shading. The tempo must flow, perhaps dotted eighth note equals 84 to 92.

The Fugue à 3

This fugue, bathed entirely in euphony, avoiding every harsh-ness, has the closest of connections with the prelude. Its subject, in which the rest signifies no separation but rather a bridge, touches the lower tonic note not at all (like that of the C Minor Fugue); it floats in the position of a triad in first inversion. Its two halves are symmetrically balanced: the motive (a) at the

beginning is turned upside down at the close; the falling pro-
gression of a fourth of the first half (b) is taken up again in the
second half and continued. These motives are already foreshadowed in the prelude, especially in the bass. Thus in the
bass line of bars 2 and 3 of the prelude (b) clearly and (a)
reshaped are to be recognized.

This reshaping of (a) is taken over in the fugue in bars 7 and 33,
where it forms the bass to the flattering figuration of the connecting section. The countersubject is also constructed from
segments of the subject, an extension and repetition of (b)
and (a).

This fugue is one of the freest, avoiding stretti and inversions,
and indeed, completely foregoing closed re-expositions, though
in the first section the exposition is followed by one complete
re-exposition (bar 11 in the soprano, bar 15 in the alto, bar 20
in the bass), which closes with a modulation to D sharp minor.
In the second section there is only one additional entry in the
alto in bar 28 and one in the soprano in bar 31, but motive (a)
comes more into play. In bar 22 Schwencke has altered this
version

to

because in strict counterpoint the connection of a shorter note
to a longer one was forbidden. Czerny went still farther:

doubtless the most flowing version, but nevertheless not by Bach. One should begin the trill in the subject with the main note in order to avoid the repetition of a note. The trill is missing in bar 12 for technical reasons, but it may be replaced with a *pralltrill*[1] (compare the E Flat Major Fugue). A suggestion for the articulation of the subject:

and of the episode:

Performance: soft and gently flowing, not lively. Quarter note equals 63 to 69.

BOOK I: NO. 14 IN F SHARP MINOR, BWV 859

This passionately tense tonality – recalling the adagio of the Sonata Opus 106 of Beethoven, the Sonata Opus 11 of Schumann – appears in Bach's instrumental works outside of *The Well-Tempered Clavier* only in the middle movements of the second Violin Sonata (BWV 1015) and the Harpsichord Concerto in A Major (BWV 1055). It appears very characteristically in the painfully unquiet mood of the tenor aria *"Ach mein Sinn"* from the Passion According to St John (BWV 245), and in the alto aria, *"Buss and Reu"* from the Passion According to St Matthew (BWV 244).

The Prelude

The key characteristics described above apply only to the fugue. The prelude leads to it, but in no way anticipates it. It seems

---

[1] The trill is quite feasible with practice. – Tr.

indifferent, indeed noncommittal; the emotional content is suppressed, hidden; one feels it only if one goes back to the prelude again from the fugue. And yet there are thematic relationships between prelude and fugue: this excerpt from the second half of the first bar has had an effect on the second full bar of the fugue's subject

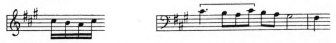

and the falling interval of a fourth b–a–g sharp–f sharp, which carries the whole prelude, creates the closing turn of the fugue subject. Without the short, continuo-type chords, this prelude could be thought of as a two-part invention; indeed, if one thinks of the lower voice as not entering until the second quarter of bar 2, it might be considered a two-voiced fugue in which, after the exposition, a second exposition in A major (bars 6–7) and a single soprano entry (bar 9) lead to the close of the first section (middle of bar 12).

In the second section there are four more entrances of the two voices: in bars 12–14, bars 14–16 (in the inversion), bars 19–20 and in the coda (bars 22–23). The wave-like flowing thirds of the subject are counterpointed with leaping eighth notes in sixths (compare the opposite procedure in the C Sharp Major Fugue); in the episodes, subject and countersubject are intermingled. Thus it is a piece of excellent proportions, which is more than merely a prelude to the fugue. But because it is also indeed a prelude, it should not be played too fleetingly, but with a certain seriousness. Quarter note equals 84.

The Fugue à 4

After this prelude, where feelings are hidden, follows one of the most expressive fugues in *The Well-Tempered Clavier*, one whose poignant effect resides equally in the subject and the countersubject. The subject rises from the tonic in three ascents of a third to the fifth: f sharp to a in quiet quarter notes, g sharp to b more pressingly in eighth notes, a sharp to c sharp' driven by the turn; it then falls again in two drops of a third (c sharp' to a and b to g sharp) back to the tonic, a model of human effort and renunciation. If there is any lingering doubt concerning the expressive intent of the subject, it vanishes when one considers the countersubject which accompanies the subject throughout the entire fugue:

This is the "sobbing" motive, well known from many of Bach's choral works (compare the Organ Chorale Prelude "*O Lamm Gottes unschuldig*," the chorus "*O Mensch bewein' dein Sünde gross*" from the St Matthew Passion [BWV 244] and the "Lament" from the Capriccio on the Departure of his Beloved Brother [BWV 992]). Both subjects together give the fugue its stamp; but yet a third motive enters which is taken from the third ascent of the subject

This has the task, with the countersubject, of supplying the few episodes of this fugue. Strange to say, as in the Fugue in F Minor, the first episode is inserted between the entry of the third and fourth voices in the exposition, so that the soprano, as there, enters only late and as the *dux*. The fugue is in two sections (bars 1 to the middle of 20, from the middle of 20 to 40) and contains in each half only a single exposition. The first section consists exclusively of the exposition and the connecting modulation to C sharp minor; the second begins with an entry of the subject in inversion in the alto on the two last quarter notes of bar 20. This entry is brought so little into relief that it can scarcely be noticed by an unprepared listener. In bar 25 the soprano follows with a reshaping of the beginning which reveals the subject only later (in regular motion):

---

[1] A tie is missing in Keller's example. – Tr.

In bar 29 the tenor enters in direct movement; in bar 32, following in his footsteps, the bass enters in contrary motion. Because
of the way the exposition is planned, the upper limit of c sharp″
is scarcely exceeded in the first part of the fugue. It breaks out
of this straightjacket in the second part and (in bar 28) reaches
a peak in the soprano and the alto, from which the upper
voices – carried by the bass with the subject in contrary movement – sink back into their opening range. A final isolated
soprano entry brings the fugue to its close. As there was no
brightening toward major in the entire movement, the major
cadence here is not a convention, but provides rather a com-
forting release of tensions. In this piece the trills, which Bach
did not write out after the entrance of the alto voice, should
be executed as *pralltrills* throughout.

Performance: serious and expressive, but not dragging; in
the countersubject the second eighth note of each pair of sighs
with a release that is somewhat shorter and softer. Quarter note
equals 96.

BOOK I: NO. 15 IN G MAJOR, BWV 860

Whereas the Viennese classics usually conceived this tonality
as quiet and thoughtful (see the Violin Sonatas of Beethoven
Opus 96 and Brahms Opus 78, and Schubert's Fantasy-Sonata
with the same opus number), with Bach it has mostly an expression of overflowing joy. This is attested by the Organ Preludes
BWV 541, 550, 568, the Fantasie, BWV 572, and among the
clavier works, the Toccata, BWV 916; all of them begin in the
same manner: with a fast, fiery run beginning on g″. The short
brilliant prelude in *The Well-Tempered Clavier* is inspired with
the same spirit.

The Prelude

Its one-part form, its brevity, its figuration built throughout
on broken chords, and its youthful exuberance place this work

among the first of the preludes contained in *The Well-Tempered Clavier*. Like some others it is transmitted to us in an earlier, shorter form through Forkel. After thirteen bars, which correspond to the current version, it closed in the following manner:

The four bars added later bring the prelude not only to an expressive climax, but intensify it as well from the point of view of texture: the sevenths which play so great a role in the fugue subject, come increasingly to the fore as characteristic intervals:

As early as bar 5 the highest notes offer the same profile as the *comes* of the fugue subject (d'–e'–f sharp'–g'–(f sharp')–b'–a'); but by the two last bars of the prelude there can no longer be any doubt about the intimate connection between the two pieces. That Bach used the time signature 24/16 for the upper staff and C for the lower staff relieved him of the necessity of marking the triplets with "3" in the opening bar.

Performance: lively and fiery, the eighth notes (with the exception of the suspensions in bars 11–13) separated. Dotted eighth note equals 80.

The Fugue à 3

A true and proper performer's fugue, whose *élan* derives from its especially rich multi-form subject (which turns about itself like a gyroscope), then with two saucy leaps reaches first the seventh, then the ninth, of the dominant, and runs back down; a fugue which was inspired by the spirit of the instrument. The exposition, it is true, is normal, as is the second exposition. in which subject and countersubject are turned upside down (alto bar 20, soprano bar 24, bass bar 28); but from then on the form is manipulated more loosely. A third exposition in minor limits itself to two voices (soprano bar 38, alto in inversion bar 43). The next entry of the subject begins a stretto (soprano bar 51, bass bar 52); however, it leaves out a bar of the subject and does not complete the stretto. With the next stretto the leading voice, the tenor (bar 60), is complete[1] but the imitating voice, the soprano (bar 61), is once more shortened. A solitary bass entry in inversion (bar 69) and an incomplete entry of the alto (bar 77), likewise inverted, introduce a stretto (bar 79) from which the soprano (which enters a third too high) emerges as victor. It leads the fugue to a triumphal close, very similar to that of the first fugue of *The Well-Tempered Clavier*. It is music, life-giving music, which creates its own laws. Characteristically the countersubject, which accommodates itself to the lines of the subject, plays no special part; not so, however, its continuation:

The eighth notes indicate an augmentation of the ending of the subject (the sixteenth notes accompany it in sixths). From these a contrary voice in the soprano, and a sustained voice in the

---

[1] The tenor is also shortened by a bar here, which Keller evidently missed. – Tr.

middle build the majority of episodes, in which the three-voiced texture is subjected to a great variety of permutations: in bars 17–19 they enter with one another as a–b–c, in bars 31–33, as c–b–a, in bars 48–50 as b–a–c and finally in bars 65–67 as c–a–b. To (c) is added in bars 34–37[1] and 73–76 a stormy scale passage in contrary motion which came to the composer certainly not through his pen but through his fingers.

The performance of this fugue requires an uninterrupted tempo, strength and fire, also something of humor (especially with the inversion of the leap of the seventh of the subject) and sharp articulation. The technically most difficult place is the inversion of the subject in the alto (bars 20–23). Czerny slurred the quarter notes in the subject c″ to b′, e″ to d″, thereby increasing the humor of the fugue; but it is false to Bach's style. Dotted quarter note equals 66 to 72.

BOOK I: NO. 16 IN G MINOR, BWV 861

If there is a key especially characteristic of the Baroque it is G minor, Handel's favorite key. Its expression is pathos, required by convention; sublimated, we find it in the great Fantasy for Organ (BWV 542) and in the Sonata for Unaccompanied Violin (BWV 1001), a high point not attained in *The Well-Tempered Clavier.*

The Prelude

This strict three-voiced, arioso prelude is reminiscent of the middle movement of a violin concerto. The solo violin (as in the middle movement of the A Minor Violin Concerto, BWV 1044) makes a slow and dignified descent from its long-held note to the tonic, modulates to B flat major and hands over the main line to the bass. A chain of no fewer than eight sequences, which leads to the close of the first half (bar 11), shows that the com-

[1] Keller: 39. – Tr.

position was indeed the work of Bach's Weimar years. Whereas in the first section the soprano has the lead, in the second the three voices have an equal share. They limit themselves to a motive which Bach also used in the two-part invention in B flat major.

This enlivens the rather inflexible rhythm of the beginning and, at the end, has the field to itself.

The player's task is to give life to the rhythm by means of an almost unnoticeable caesura (always after the first sixteenth note) in bars 2, 4–6 and 8, and to inspire the whole somewhat conventional piece through a *cantabile* quality modelled on the tone of the violin. The expressive trills in bars 1, 3, 7 and 11 should not be played metrically, but rather as directed by Frescobaldi in the preface to his *Fiori Musicali*, beginning slowly, then increasing their speed, and toward the end slackening again. The tempo is a quiet, not dragging *andante*. Quarter note equals 44.

The Fugue à 4

In its subject this fugue makes use of a model common in Baroque music for which Max Seiffert has worked out a whole pedigree in his *Geschichte der Klaviermusik* (History of Clavier Music). The immediate model for Bach was probably the subject of the E Flat Major Fugue in Fischer's *Ariadne Musica*:

The fugue is four-voiced, but it makes use of four-voice texture only in bars 15–18 and in the coda (from bar 28) (in the next-to-last bar a second tenor enters with the subject as a "fifth voice" and this statement brings the fugue to an end). The soprano rests from the middle of bar 6 to bar 15,[1] the tenor from bar 19 to 28. This is as little characteristic of a master fugue as the line of the countersubject,

which in its first half uses the consequent of the subject, and in its second half uses the antecedent of the subject and inverts it. David sees in this an advantage, because "euphony, balance, ingenuity have been blended." But one could equally well assert that because of this treatment the fugue keeps churning round in a circle. Twice it lifts itself to greatness: in the stretto of bass and alto in bars 17–18, where the widely spaced voices can barely be encompassed by the player's fingers, and in the coda with its strettos of soprano, tenor and bass (bars 28–29[2]) to which the alto adds the countersubject.

   The player must not let the subject fall apart into statement and answer but bridge the rest. Quietly moving tempo. Quarter note equals 56.

BOOK I: NO. 17 IN A FLAT MAJOR, BWV 862

This key, very familiar to us from the Romantic period, appears very rarely in the Baroque even though it is used as early as Pachelbel and J. K. F. Fischer; but Bach, apart from *The Well-Tempered Clavier*, never uses it in his instrumental works, not even in middle movements. In the St Matthew Passion (BWV 224) he uses it several times for the expression of dark solemnity ("*Wahrlich, dieser ist Gottes Sohn gewesen*" – Truly this was the Son of God) ("*Ach, Golgotha*" – Ah, Golgotha).

The Prelude

This prelude increases the variety of forms of the preludes of *The Well-Tempered Clavier* with a new type: it has the form of

---

[1] Keller: 14. – Tr.   [2] Keller says "27–28" here. – Tr.

a small Baroque concerto movement, a form which Bach, from his Cöthen years on, made use of especially in preludes in the grand style; for example, in the Organ Preludes in C Minor, C Major, B Minor, E Flat Major (BWV 546, 547, 544, 552), in the outer movements of the Italian Concerto (BWV 971), and in some preludes to the English Suites (BWV 806 to 811). Chief sections and subsidiary sections alternate as in the *Grosso* and *Concertino*; the circle of keys which the chief subject passes through is generally confined to the usual tonic–dominant–subdominant–tonic; the subsidiary sections intervene between these chief sections. In the A Flat Major Prelude the turn to the subdominant is missing. It has the form A (bars 1–9) – B (bars 9–18)–A (bars 18–22)–B (bars 22–35)–A (bars 35–44).

A copy once possessed by Forkel gives an alternative, obviously earlier version of bars 9–12 and 22–26.

The form which Bach has given this prelude excludes the lyrical conception which is found in many editions. It is festive, somewhat ceremonial, and it is related to the fugue through the way in which the subjects of both circumscribe the triad. The harmonic succession, tonic–dominant–tonic in the prelude contrasts with the tonic–subdominant–tonic of the fugue subject. The leap B flat–a flat in bar 37 in the bass, a doubling of the seventh, a flat', in the upper voice, was corrected by Kirnberger in analogy with bar 35, to read B flat–b flat. The player should give special attention to the independent phrasing of the two voices. Thus, for example, in bars 10–12 there should be a light separation in the bass after the first eighth note, and of the upper voice after the fifth sixteenth note; chief sections and subsidiary sections require terraced dynamics. Quarter note equals 72.

The Fugue à 4

This fugue turns the forces of the prelude inward; it has an indescribable nobility and warmth, but it seems to have been written more for the organ than the clavier; indeed one could imagine it as a choral fugue in a Mass (perhaps for the *Sanctus*).

Its subject, built only from broken triads fitted together, establishing a connection with the prelude, foregoes highly individual traits, as does also the countersubject, which juxtaposes a delicate movement in seconds to the harmonic steps of the subject. It ends on a tied appoggiatura which, combined with the transformed sixteenth notes of the countersubject and the eighth notes of the subject, form the three-voiced episodes:

In ceremonial calm these fall sequentially downwards (bars 11–12, 13–14, 19–22 and 25–26), and only at the end raise themselves to a large climax (which Bach might have carried further to d flat''' and e flat''' if the range of the keyboard had permitted); then the voices fall, and the soprano, accompanied by unpretentious chords (compare the close of the D Sharp Minor Fugue in Book II) concludes the fugue in humility. Its form is handled with surpassing freedom notwithstanding its severe mien. Only one complete re-exposition of all four voices is juxtaposed to the exposition (bars 27–31, bass bar 27, tenor bar 28, alto bar 29, soprano bar 30); in between, the subject is stated in just two voices on three occasions (bars 10 and 13, bars 17–18 and bars 23–24). Through the tonal answer the subject loses its harmonic significance and it is also repeatedly altered (bars 18, 23–24, 24–25). An upbeat reading (with a caesura after the third eighth note) would destroy its peace, for the entire fugue requires a continuous legato and provides only a few pauses for breath. The tempo should be solemnly slow, although not dragging. Quarter note equals 44 to 48.

BOOK I: NO. 18 IN G SHARP MINOR, BWV 863

The key of G Sharp Minor appears very rarely in either the Classic period or the Romantic period (Chopin, Étude in thirds); Bach never uses it outside *The Well-Tempered Clavier*. Since the G Sharp Minor pieces in Book I and Book II were probably composed in G minor and subsequently transposed, there is no evidence that this key had any special significance for Bach.

The Prelude

This prelude, like its successor, is a three-part invention, the first one in *The Well-Tempered Clavier*. The essence of an invention, namely the development of a subject (of an "*inventio*") without the addition of further motives or subjects, is here illustrated in exemplary manner. The subject is a characteristic metric motive built from sixteenth and eighth notes. It is stated in the soprano, imitated by the bass, then carried on in the soprano with a sequential remodelling of its first half (bars 3–4). The device is then repeated, first between alto and bass (bars 5–6), then in bars 8–9 between alto[1] and soprano so that thereby all three possible combinations have been utilized. In bar 10 the subject enters in inversion; in bar 14 the first part of the prelude comes to an end. The second part overlaps it with the bass entry in bar 13; again an inversion of the sixteenth notes, then the sixteenth notes as well as the eighth notes are spun out sequentially (bars 18–21). In bars 22–23 the first motive alone is treated in stretto, then three bars lead to the coda with an organpoint in the soprano. The intensification of measures 18 to 24 is underlined by the "double stops" in bar 24 and the passionate diminished seventh chord in bar 25, and then brought to an end. A motivic reference to the fugue subject is hinted at in the first three notes of the soprano and in the bass of the two first bars (g sharp–f double sharp–g sharp–a sharp–b).

The player should remember that for Bach the chief aim of the inventions was "to attain a *cantabile* manner in performance." This charming piece, therefore, avoiding strong accents, requires a *cantabile* performance which inspires all voices; to

---

[1] Keller here says "between the bass and soprano so that thereby all three possible combinations have been utilized." He is stretching a point – the instances are not precisely parallel. Actually the subject here comes in the bass, soprano and alto in that order in bars 7, 8 and 9. – Tr.

achieve this a quietly moving tempo is called for, with eighth notes as the metric unit. Eighth note equals 96.

The Fugue à 4

If it is the purpose of a prelude to lead to the stricter form of the fugue, here the case is inverted: after a strictly worked prelude there follows one of the freest fugues of *The Well-Tempered Clavier*. The cause of this is found in its subject, which is so rich in individual traits that it can be subjected to no routine fugal process. It has almost romantic characteristics: its first note is a lengthened upbeat eighth note (which only appears in its true form in bar 37). Yet it holds back the movement which gently surrounds the tonic note; then the line stretches through a rising tritone (the only one among all the fugue subjects of Bach) to reach the fifth. This note is reinterpreted as the octave of the dominant, from which the theme charmingly, somewhat self-satisfiedly sinks to the tonic with the repeated eighth notes. After the subjects in D Minor, E Flat Major, E Major, E Minor, this is the fifth fugue subject in *The Well-Tempered Clavier* which modulates to the dominant. The *comes* follows the return route to the tonic immediately after its first tone via the subdominant. Two countersubjects are added to the subject. The first adapts itself to the subject

the second can be considered as an augmentation of the beginning of the subject (not carried through consistently):

From this line used as a middle voice, the repeated eighth notes in the bass, and the first countersubject in the soprano, the playful episodes which give the fugue its stamp are constructed:

A second type of episode utilizes an excerpt from the subject
with the interval of the tritone (bars 21–23[1] and 28 to 30):

After a strict beginning, the structure of this fugue becomes
progressively more and more relaxed. To the exposition is added
an additional entry in the tenor as *comes* (bar 11). Then two
re-expositions, one of three voices (bass bar 15, tenor bar 17,
alto bar 19) and another of only two voices (soprano bar 24,
bass bar 26), are followed by two further single entries by the
tenor (bar 32) and soprano (bar 37). This is all achieved with
ease and some humor; only the tenor entry in bar 32 is somewhat unfortunately crowded. To avoid the cross relation with
the alto, Bach had to raise b to b sharp, but was obliged in so
doing to accept the cross relation with b′ in the soprano. This is
the only fugue in the first book of *The Well-Tempered Clavier*
which closes in minor – showing in this too its "modern"
character.

Performance: expressive, but with grace. The subject is
legato except for the repeated eighth notes, which are lightly
separated. Quarter note equals 63.

BOOK I: NO. 19 IN A MAJOR, BWV 864

The light, spring-like quality which Mozart often gives to
A major is also found in Bach, as witness the idyllic Prelude and
Fugue for Organ (BWV 536) and the First English Suite (BWV
806). But Bach does not stress this aspect of the key in *The Well-
Tempered Clavier*; in the prelude the interest is primarily contrapuntal, and the fugue is problematic in more than one
respect. Nor is there a motivic or inner relationship between
the movements.

[1] Keller: 25. – Tr.

The Prelude

Like the preceding prelude, this is a three-part invention, but more artful in developing three themes in triple counterpoint in much the same way as the three-part invention in F Minor, with which it even shares its third subject in descending quarter notes. The progress of the movement is shaped by the opening theme, whose falling sequences are accompanied by the syncopations of the second subject,

while the third, in quiet quarter-note movement, chromatically falls first, then imitates the steps of a fifth of the second subject:

Of the six possible combinations of the three subjects, four are brought to use in six expositions: a–b–c at the beginning and (in the minor, with an octave transposition of the beginning) bars 12–14; a–c–b in bars 20–22; b–c–a in bars 4–6, and the middle of bar 17–19; and c–a–b from the middle of bar 8–11. The six subject complexes divide themselves into two groups of three each (bars 1–12 and 12–24). The short episodes just prepare the entries of the subject (bars 6 to the middle of 8 and bars 14 to the middle of 17). The eighth-note motive of the episodes,

as well as the sixteenth-note motive of the bass is taken from the beginning of the subject, so that a concentrated unity of musical material is created. With such compactness of form we are no longer justified in speaking of its "prelude-like" character.

In order to distinguish the three subjects in performance, the performer may accent the first note of the second subject and release the second note lightly; in the third subject slur together the chromatic notes and the leaps of a fifth. Quiet, reflective tempo. Quarter note equals 66.

The Fugue à 3

This fugue contrasts the dance rhythm of a 9/8 bar with the moderate common time of the prelude. Its subject is the strangest in the whole of *The Well-Tempered Clavier*: a single eighth note, followed after three rests by fourths clambering busily upward, ending with a modulation to the dominant. (The cadential note e″ at the beginning of the third bar is avoided in the first entry because it would have created the interval of a fourth with the lower voice b′.) Since the subject modulates to the dominant, the *comes* leads (as in the G Sharp Minor Fugue) back to the tonic immediately after its first note. Almost as peculiar as the subject is the structure of the fugue: two parts of equal length, the first in eighth-note, the second in sixteenth-note, movement (bars 1–20 and 21–41). The coda which follows repeats both parts in shortened form (bars 42[1]–48 and 49–54), giving the movement an A B a b form.

In the first part there is no regular countersubject, the fourths of the subject being continually treated in stretto. The exposition contains four entries, for the bass enters twice (the first time in the range of the tenor). A second exposition consists of three entries (soprano bar 9, bass bar 13, bass in the tenor position bar 16).

In the second part, the sixteenth-note countersubject introduces new life into the fugue and releases us from the endless movement of fourths. Without any episode, it attaches itself to the subject, which undergoes the most varied transformations.

[1] Keller: 41. – Tr.

Thus in bars 29 and 30 the fourths are extended to sixths; the soprano in bar 30 should really be led to d''' (to which Spitta has already called attention):

The subject, which throughout the entire fugue makes no further unaltered entrance in the soprano after the entry in bar 9, is shifted by an eighth note in bars 25–26:

so that here a stretto of all three voices takes place. In the double coda (from bar 42) the subject enters only twice, in the alto (bar 42) and bass (bar 44).

This fugue has been viewed in a variety of ways by its editors: Czerny provided the first note with a *ff* like a starting shot before the race; Riemann finds it 'of the most subjective expression and an almost touching *naïveté*'; Tovey conceives it as 'a delicate and complicated *scherzo*.' If indeed the first part is not entirely serious, nevertheless the second part and the conclusion crown this 'complicated *scherzo*,' as Tovey rightly describes it. The tempo can be the same as in the prelude. Dotted quarter note equals 66.

BOOK I: NO. 20 IN A MINOR, BWV 865

How Bach conceived this tonality – masculine, loaded with energy – he showed in a whole number of works: the great Organ Prelude with Fugue (BWV 543), the Sonata for Violin Unaccompanied (BWV 1003), the Triple Concerto (BWV 1044), and equally clearly in the two fugues of *The Well-Tempered Clavier*. But how does this fugue of the first volume get into *The Well-Tempered Clavier*, in which it does not belong at all? That it must have been conceived before the first Cöthen years of Bach is shown by the sustained A at the end which was only playable on the pedals of an organ or pedal harpsichord. Such isolated pedal notes are found in certain youthful works of Bach, but later not at all. Moreover, its unusual length shows that it could not have been composed for *The Well-Tempered Clavier*; equally its style proclaims it to be an early work of Bach. Thus we have here a parallel with the Prelude in E Flat Major, which we have recognized as a preamble with a double fugue, and the D Sharp (E Flat) Minor Fugue. This large-scale, significant fugue, in common with the others just mentioned, exemplifies a still not fully achieved mastery. Especially close to it stands the E Flat Minor Fugue, in that both of them cannot do enough in the art of inversion and stretto. Is it an accident that the E Flat Minor Fugue in the first half of *The Well-Tempered Clavier* stands in the same place as the A Minor Fugue in the second?

The Prelude

Bach faced the task of creating a prelude to this great fugue, 'strutting along in full armor' (Spitta), which would not only serve as preparation but, through a completely contrasting mood, rise to an importance of its own. The introduction to the great Fugue in A Minor (BWV 944) in 3/4 time makes no attempt at this individual significance; here however Bach chooses as a contrast to the somewhat ponderous C-measure of the fugue, a dance-like, moving 9/8 meter, in this way reversing the relationship of the two movements when compared with the A Major Prelude and Fugue. The elastically resilient subject of this prelude is developed with the regularity of a dance movement in four-bar phrases: four bars in the tonic, an equal number in the dominant, and four bars of transition back to C major. Further, four bars of the subject in C major and five bars of return lead to a shortened recapitulation of 4 plus 4 bars (the closing bar counted doubled). The prelude is, in spite of its brevity, in no way insignificant; rather, in the free, unconstrained mastery of its medium, it is superior to the fugue. Bach has made no attempt at a thematic connection between prelude and fugue. Dotted quarter note equals 66.

The Fugue à 4

Why, one may ask, did Bach choose this fugue for *The Well-Tempered Clavier*, when there were several shorter A minor fugues ready at hand among earlier works (BWV 895, 904, 947)? Obviously the contents of these did not satisfy him, so he selected this one, the longest in Book I: it numbers 87[1] C bars with sixteenth-note movement (the D Sharp Minor Fugue, 87 bars in eighth-note movement; the C Sharp Minor Fugue, 115 c measures; the B Minor Fugue, 76 C bars). Its subject Bach used again later, slightly altered, when he made it the basis of the opening chorus in his Cantata '*Bisher habt ihr nichts gebeten in meinem Namen*' (BWV 87), composed in 1735. Its measured rhythm expresses firmness, an expression which rises to pathos in the declamatory break on the third, g sharp to e. Thus this fugue tells us at once in its subject what it intends. With its well-considered, rational design, it intends to be a proving ground in which all the possibilities of stretto, inversion, and a combination of both will be exercised so thoroughly that it could stand as an example of these techniques in any manual of fugal composition. As a result, it cannot entirely avoid giving a didactic impression; it is just such a work, but that of a genius. In relation to the B Flat Minor Fugue in Book II, composed much later, it is an apprentice work compared to a masterpiece.

It consists of six expositions (the same number as in the E Flat Minor Fugue), which are built upon one another to an exact plan. The first exposition proceeds as far as the middle of bar 14 (alto, soprano, bass, tenor), and is connected directly to the second exposition with the subject in inversion (middle of bar 14 to middle of 27) in the order soprano (bar 14), tenor (bar 18), bass (bar 21) and alto (bar 24). Each voice enters on the second or sixth eighth note of the bar in a way which does not make it easy for eye or ear to recognize it. The third exposition follows immediately (middle of bar 27 to 40[2]). Here the subject

---

[1] Keller: 85. – Tr.   [2] Keller: to the middle of 39. – Tr.

in its original form is treated in stretto at the octave at half a bar's distance. In this manner are bundled together: soprano and tenor (bars 27–28), alto and bass (bars 31–32), tenor and alto (bars 36–37). Only now is there room for the first episode, in which there is a modulation to C major (bars 40^1–42). In the fourth exposition (bars 43–65) the subject, now in the major, is treated in stretto between soprano and bass (bar 43), then between alto and tenor in inversion (bars 48–49), similarly between bass and soprano (bar 53), and finally between soprano and alto (bars 57–58). In this final stretto Bach is obliged to alter the leap of a third in the alto in bar 59 to a fourth (f sharp' to b').[2] These four connected expositions conclude in the upper voices in bar 65 (here for the first time one sees rests in the music), overlapping the fifth exposition which has already begun in the middle of bar 64: bass and tenor are treated in stretto at the interval of the fifth. The soprano and alto follow, at the fifth below, in bars 67–68. There is a modulation to F major (bars 70–72). The last, sixth, exposition brings first the bass and soprano in stretto (in the manner anticipated in the fourth exposition). Bach now winds up toward the final climax with a three-part stretto: the tenor in inversion (bar 76) is followed one bar later by the alto at the interval of the ninth (!) culminating with the soprano (the leading of whose line is altered), and the breaking off of all voices on the third inversion of a seventh chord (bar 80). Such an emphatic pause on a dissonance – of which the most powerful example comes at the close of the organ Passacaglia in C Minor (BWV 582), and another at the end of the great C Major Fugue for Organ (BWV 547) – serves to enhance the pathos of the final cadence. But to the young Bach a single pause was insufficient here: after two bars in which the alto and soprano are strettoed at the fifth, a second breaking off follows on the second inversion of a seventh chord on the second dominant,[3] accompanied by powerful chords of the now five-voiced structure. The way is now open for an organpoint on the tonic, over which Bach introduces a final stretto, excelling everything that has gone before, of four voices in two pairs: bass and tenor in contrary

[1] Keller: 39. – Tr.
[2] Keller here says f sharp to b flat. – Tr.
[3] Keller: dominant. – Tr.

motion with soprano and alto. In the final bar the thirds increase the structure to seven voices.

This description is not an analysis, but rather a prosaic outline which will give the reader and player a first look into the structure of this powerful fugue. This is perhaps not entirely unnecessary, because it is not always easy to recognize the subject entries as such, since they are not prepared through rests, and the reader and listener are distracted by numerous false entries. What the fugue lacks is a relaxation through episodes with fewer voices. The structure is four-voiced almost throughout, and moves with regular compactness through the middle range of the instrument. Above all the monotony of the rhythm produces in the end an effect of stagnation.

The player should not emphasize all the entries of the subject; it is more important to separate the large sections from one another. A second performer may well play (with octave doubling) the organpoint at the end, best begun as early as bar 83. Quarter note equals 66 (like the prelude).

BOOK I: NO. 21 IN B FLAT MAJOR, BWV 866

The key of B Flat Major, lying stepwise a wholetone below C, is stamped in our imagination especially through certain great works of Beethoven: the Sonatas Opus 22 and 106, the Fourth Symphony. Bach used it only very rarely and conceived it in almost neutral fashion (Partita No. 1, BWV 825, the Sixth Brandenburg Concerto, BWV 1051). In both parts of *The Well-Tempered Clavier* it has the character of cheerfulness and grace.

The Prelude

This prelude, the shortest in length in *The Well-Tempered Clavier*, and technically one of the most brilliant, is a rapidly and lightly tossed-off little toccata, which in spite of its brevity displays the essential characteristics of its type: broken harmonies, virtuoso passage work divided between the hands, punctuated by massive, full chords. In the topmost notes of the prelude and in the bass, the fugue subject is already lightly sketched: d''–c''–d''–f'' becomes in the fugue subject with its upbeat opening f'–g'–f'–b flat'. The sharing of the passage work between the hands reminds one of the organ (as does the jagged bass in the beginning); cf. the beginning of the C Major Toccata (bwv 564), the so-called 'Little' E Minor Prelude (bwv 533) and the G Minor Fantasy (bwv 542). In all these examples the line, through its division between the hands, becomes not only more brilliant, but also receives a more inward liveliness. It is worth noting that the passages in bars 11–14, which relax the chords, have not been so divided. An authentic copy has the full-voiced chords marked *adagio*, a reading which almost all editions have adopted but which signifies only a scarcely noticeable, almost obvious broadening. At the close, after the upward floating figure, in one manuscript (and unfortunately also with Czerny) a whole note B flat has been added in the bass which not only lacks all credibility, but exactly reverses Bach's obvious intention. The fermata on the last note (b flat'') which is missing in many copies, is only here to mark the close.

The performance may be free, as is appropriate to a toccata: but with too much license, so short a piece may fall apart. As a basic tempo, one may take quarter note equals 69.

The Fugue à 3

This fugue is in the nature of a strict dance, of an almost capricious grace, a sort of after-dance, a *proportio tripla* to the prelude. Its light steps become more nimble in the second bar and carry over in the third and fourth into a whirling movement (structure of the subject: a a b b). The mood is further intensified by two regular countersubjects. The first one

paraphrases the first two bars of the subject and provides a tambourine-like beat to the two following bars; the second

is content with short, impertinent interjections. The character of the subject and the presence of two countersubjects puts this fugue in the same category as those in C Minor and C Sharp Major; the structure of the subject ($1 + 1 + 2 = 4$ bars) is especially like that of the C Minor Fugue, and makes it almost inevitable that here again artful fugal devices are avoided. It is in two sections; the first (bars 1–22) consists of the exposition and an additional entry of the soprano as *comes* (bar 13); the second (bars 22–48), of two incomplete expositions of two voices each: alto and bass (bars 22 and 26 in G minor – C minor), soprano and alto (bars 37 and 41 in E flat major – B flat major). The subject is always present, even in the episodes, which twice make five-bar interruptions between the thematic passages (bars 17–21 and 30–34), while everything else flows in a normal four-measure pattern.

The eighth notes are an inversion of (a), the sixteenths refer to (b). The excitement of the end of the fugue is heightened by the repetition of bars 43 and 44, not least because here its already considerable technical demands are increased (a fugue which Riemann numbered among the easiest and most unassuming!).

The false entry of the subject in the alto (bar 35) is one of those jokes in which this fugue abounds.

For the understanding of this fugue not much need be said, for all is clear; but the contrary is the case concerning its performance. How should one articulate the subject? According to Czerny

(that is the most common and perhaps the conception most suitable to the *scherzando* character of the fugue). Other editors suggest

Kreutz rejects both as not in the style of Bach and suggests that all eighth notes be separated, the sixteenth notes played with a "pearly" quality. The notes of the first countersubject should be individually articulated.

The two-voiced passages particularly in the left hand incorporating the second countersubject (bars 15–18 and 39–40), give many players difficulty as one knows from experience. To avoid cramping the hand, the eighth notes might be played with light finger staccato. In bars 45–46 (which are simplified in a copy from Forkel) the sixths should be given entirely to the right hand.

Performance: with caprice and humor, with a lively dance rhythm. Quarter note equals 96.

BOOK I: NO. 22 IN B FLAT MINOR, BWV *867*

The dark, heavily veiled tonality of B Flat Minor was not first expounded by Chopin in his Sonata Opus 35, but appeared earlier with Carl Phillip Emanuel Bach in an "*Adagio assai mesto e sostenuto*," and with Bach himself in the duet "*In deine Hände befehle ich meinen Geist*" from the Cantata BWV 106 (*Actus tragicus*). This prelude and fugue in *The Well-Tempered Clavier* are imbued with the same spirit.

The Prelude

In this prelude the heavy dragging rhythm of the upper voices and the monotonous, ostinato eighth notes of the bass give us the impression of marching along in a funeral procession. Again we are reminded of the introduction to the *Actus tragicus*, with its two recorders, two gambas and basso continuo (an instrumentation one could also imagine for this prelude in *The Well-Tempered Clavier*):

Here, as there, the structure is five-voiced, decreasing to four voices, only to increase at the close to nine real voices in the shattering outburst on the diminished seventh chord a–c–e flat–g flat, the outcry of a frightened soul. This chord, so much used in later music and soon worn out, first appeared in music about 1700, and Bach was one of the first who recognized its elemental effect. Of this we have evidence in the D Minor Toccata for Organ (BWV 565), then here in *The Well-Tempered Clavier*, and later in the eight-voiced "*Barrabas!*" from the St Matthew Passion (BWV 244). After the fermata, the prelude ends in major, but not delicately (Czerny), *diminuendo al pp* but rather serious and collected. Its structure is two-part (bars 1–12 and 13–24), and moreover the 12 bars of each half are regularly subdivided. It is better to think of the subject not as a patchwork of little motives, but rather as a long line, constructed from linked phrases:

The tempo is that of a slow step, while the strict form objectifies the expression of suppressed pathos which should not be diminished into weakness or sentimentality. Quarter note equals 50 to 54.

The Fugue á 5

In few pieces of *The Well-Tempered Clavier* is the inner unity of prelude and fugue so convincing as here. Both reveal the same traits of suffering, both begin with five voices, reducing the number of voices, only to increase them again later, the prelude to the breaking-off on the diminished seventh chord, the fugue to the high point of a fivefold stretto. The subject, a pure choral subject (perhaps on *Christe Eleison*), is characterized by the dissonance of the minor ninth (f to g flat''); its continuation serves as countersubject. The five voices are usually interpreted as though for soprano, alto, tenor I and II, and bass; they are better conceived as soprano I and II, alto, tenor and bass.

In the other five-voiced fugue of *The Well-Tempered Clavier*, in C Sharp Minor, the voices are introduced from the bass in rising order; in the B Flat Minor Fugue, the order is reversed: the soprano I begins, the bass enters as the last voice. This relationship can hardly be accidental, as both fugues are symmetrical to each other in *The Well-Tempered Clavier*: the C Sharp Minor Fugue a half step above C (the first tonality), the B Flat Minor Fugue a half step below B (the last tonality). As in the E Major and F Major Fugues, the end of the subject of the B Flat Minor Fugue cannot be precisely fixed. Intrinsically, it ends only at the beginning of bar 4, but it is often used, especially in stretti, in a shortened form. As in a choral fugue of Handel, at the beginning the two sopranos twist ever higher, so that the alto can first enter only at bar 10; the tenor follows, again in stretto, in bar 12, the bass in bar 15.[1] Riemann wished to rewrite the fugue in 4/2 meter, but the many metric irregularities prevent that. Like the prelude, the fugue is in two sections (bars 1–37 and 37–75[2]). The two sopranos are silent from bar 37 to 50, where they enter again in stretto; the alto drops out from bar 56 to 68. The two stretti bar 50 and bar 52–53 (of bass and tenor) and the organpoint bar 62 prepare the stretto of all five voices at the distance of a half note, a stretto probably unique, notwithstanding a predecessor in the fourfold stretto at the close of the Organ Fugue in B Minor (BWV 579). From the point of sound, it does not come off successfully on a keyboard instrument, and even to read it two staves are too few; only the full score makes it clear:[3]

---

[1] Keller: 18. – Tr.   [2] Keller: 73. – Tr.

[3] Although it is extremely difficult to do so, I believe that this stretto can be made to sound, and in order to prepare it, I use an articulation which separates the half notes at the beginning of the subject quite distinctly. Then when, at this stretto they enter in rapid succession, their separation makes it possible for the ear to hear them out individually and to follow their continuation as the voices resume in quarter notes. – Tr.

When after this powerful compression the fugue ends in the major,[1] it signifies a triumph: '*Tod, wo ist dein Stachel, Hölle, wo ist dein Sieg?*' ('Death, where is thy sting, Hell, where is thy victory?').

Performance: song-like throughout, with the fullness and warmth of choral sound: the rest in the subject must be bridged over otherwise the expression of the ninth is weakened. The tempo is similar to that of the prelude. Half note equals 50 to 54.

BOOK I: NO. 23 IN B MAJOR, BWV 868

Bach seems to have assigned no special color value to this key, which with him occurs only once more outside *The Well-Tempered Clavier*, in the Passepied II of the French Overture (BWV 831). Apparently both pieces were composed in B flat major. If one accepts this hypothesis, then the relationship of this prelude with the first Partita (BWV 825) is striking. Here is also the only instance where the thematic relationship of prelude and fugue is openly apparent.

The Prelude

This prelude, like its predecessors in G sharp minor and A major, is a three-part invention. It presents itself more unassumingly, but with what art is this masterly little piece created from a single motive – the sixteenth notes of the first half bar! Its structure has the harmonic proportion of $5+4\frac{1}{2}+4\frac{1}{2}+5=19$ bars. In the last section the number of voices is increased to four, in the final bar to five, and here, after the sixteenth-note motive has hinted at the first half of the fugue subject so clearly, we hear the second half in the thirds of the upper voice:

[1] It doesn't continue in the major; it does emphasize several dominants and cadences in the major. – Tr.

The euphony of the voice leading is clouded only in one place, in bar 11.

In two manuscripts the alto, by analogy with bar 12, is improved;

nevertheless the first version stands in the autograph copy and an error in Bach's handwriting is unlikely.

As an aid to its performance one may think of a delicate woodwind sound, the tempo quietly flowing. Here again the rests in the subject must be bridged over, the movement carried through them. Quarter note equals 72 to 80.

The Fugue à 4

Generally, this fugue has not been counted among the most significant in *The Well-Tempered Clavier*. This is due first to its plagal subject, which in exclusively scalewise steps reaches a fourth above and below the tonic note; also the next-to-the-last half note greatly hinders the flow of the motion. It has, however, its own beauties, which do not lie open to view. Among these must be reckoned the harmoniousness of its formal plan. It consists of two parts of equal length (bars 1–17 and 18–34) each with a complete exposition and an exposition consisting of only two entries, in the first part, of the tenor (bar 11) and alto (bar 16); in the second part, of the alto (bar 29) and soprano (bar 31). The two complete expositions are exactly the same length (bars 1–8 and 18–25 with a cadential note in the next bar) and are separated from the next entry through equally long episodes (bars 9–11 and 26–28). The chief charm of this fugue, however, is created by the two inversions of the subject entering unexpectedly in the highest position of the soprano (bar 18) and the alto (bar 20). Both radiate a warmth which the other voices share, especially the bass and tenor, which enter in normal movement. Finally the soprano enters in high position and leads the fugue to a delicate close on the third, a unique feature in the major fugues of Book I of *The Well-Tempered Clavier*. For all this one begins to love it and to value it indeed.

The performance should be quiet and song-like in all the voices. One can preserve the trill of the subject as a *pralltrill* throughout the fugue. Quarter note equals 60.

BOOK I: NO. 24 IN B MINOR, BWV 869

The key of B minor, which stands at the tense interval of a major seventh to C major, has been strikingly neglected in the Viennese classics; Chopin and Liszt first presented its passion in grand style in their two piano sonatas. In two late works Bach gave it consecration, in his Mass (BWV 232) and in the great Organ Prelude and Fugue (BWV 544). To these, the last piece of Book I of *The Well-Tempered Clavier* is a worthy partner. Bach already makes it extraordinarily conspicuous by providing prelude and fugue with tempo indications. Also, in its style the prelude assumes a special position, as does the fugue, with its subject which contains all 12 half-tone steps of the scale. From the point of view of their significance, both are worthy to conclude and to crown Bach's great work.

The Prelude

Like a pre-Classic sonata movement, this prelude consists of two parts of unequal length, both to be repeated, although the second part contains no recapitulation of the first. Here we may notice influences from Bach's chamber music. In the Sonatas for Violin and Obbligato Harpsichord (BWV 1014 and 1019), conceived perhaps at the same time, there is a series of movements that are purely three-voiced, the first melodic voice assigned to the solo instrument, the second to the right hand, and the bass to the left hand of the harpsichord. The classicist of this technique was Arcangelo Corelli with his 48 Trio Sonatas for two violins and figured bass. But whereas Bach, in his sonatas, gave a share of the thematic interest to the bass, with Corelli the bass still has a purely supporting role, frequently in continuous eighth-note movement, over which the two upper voices are led imitatively. This technique was Bach's model in the B Minor Prelude. The two upper voices proceed in close imitation above the quietly moving bass. Also the motive of the rising fourth, which is syncopated and falls back to a third, is the general property of Italian chamber music at the beginning of the eighteenth century. Where, however, Bach greatly exceeds his models is in the breadth of the line which is built from this little motive. Three such lines are built in the first part of the prelude (bars 1 to the middle of 7, middle of 7 to bar 12, and bars 12–17). In the first section (B minor to D major) the alto leads, the soprano following closely on its heels at the distance of a fifth; in the second section (D major to F sharp minor) the soprano leads, the alto following a fourth lower; in the third section (F sharp minor to D major) the alto leads, the soprano following at the fifth above.[1] In this last section there is no suggestion of the usual recapitulation; but rather we can admire Bach's art of transforming a subject: the motive of a fourth is first diminished to eighth notes,

then in bars 27 and 29 broadened to a diminished fifth

and in bars 31–32 is led downward sequentially. From here on it is broadened and extended in the alto melodically

---

[1] Keller has an omission here in his original text. – Tr.

and led sequentially to the heights (bars 33–35), where with the soprano in stretto (bars 36–38) it rises ever higher before descending in syncopation to the final cadence (bars 39 to the middle of 42). Here the prelude could well end, but Bach evades the close and adds a coda which ingeniously established the connection of the diatonic prelude with the chromatic fugue: the motive of a fourth is transformed and chromaticized (middle of 42 to the middle of 45),

the bass also is led chromatically (bars 43–44). In the soprano and alto we hear in bar 43 b'–a sharp' and g'–f sharp', in bar 44 e''–d sharp'' and b'–a sharp', in bar 45 g''–f sharp'' as anticipation of the suspension motive of the fugue subject. They open the gate through which we will enter into the wonderful structure of the last fugue. The prelude, a model example of the legato style,[1] is best presented from an acoustic point of view on an organ with two manuals.

In performance on the piano one may bring out whichever voice leads at the moment, then the imitating voice will also stand out clearly. The repetitions should be played enabling the size of the prelude to stand in the correct relationship to the fugue. Bach's direction *andante* does not mean as in the case of the Romantics a preliminary stage to *adagio*, but rather a quiet, steady tempo, perhaps quarter note equals 69.

The Fugue à 4

This great fugue with which Bach concludes his work – in its duration the longest of *The Well-Tempered Clavier* – has a signific-

---

[1] My own approach to the articulation of this work is to detach slightly the opening fourth of the motive, and to emphasize the syncopated note, which makes for hearing out the imitations more easily. It is also effective to detach all the bass notes slightly, even though Keller sees this as 'a model example of the legato style.' – Tr.

ance among his clavier fugues similar to that of the first *Kyrie* Fugue of the B Minor Mass (BWV 232) in his church music. Both are alike not only in their inner attitude, but also in the structure of their subjects.

The subject from the Mass has the same motives in seconds, although in the Mass subject, the resolution of the half-step movement is, more vigorously, on the accented part of the beat and here it is on the unaccented part of the beat. The Mass subject has at its command the sacredness of the text of the Mass, the chorus, and orchestra; the clavier fugue must express what it has to say with the modest means of a sober keyboard instrument. But this very asceticism gives it a more severe effect, making greater demands on performer and hearer alike. Its subject places, between two broken triads as corner pillars, the 'sigh-motive,' suspensions released on the note of the resolution. These suspensions are not led further downwards as in the F Sharp Minor Fugue, but rise in passionate intensification, harmonically traversing the road from the tonic via the sub-dominant to the dominant. As in the fugues in F Minor, F Sharp Minor and B Major, the penultimate note has a trill, abandoned here after the first entry. The harmonic richness of the subject is as great as the melodic; it contains all 12 notes of the chromatic octave (the tonic note and the fifth three times, the third twice), and travels from the tonic via the dominant, subdominant, and second dominant to the close on the dominant.

This bold subject, laden with *Affekts*, surrounds itself with several satellites: first with the countersubject which accompanies it in quarter notes throughout the entire fugue with relentless harshness,

then with a bridge motive to the countersubject,

which enters in inversion in the soprano in bar 9; similarly bar 13 in the tenor, bar 21 in the bass (in direct movement), bars 34–35 in the tenor, bar 39 in inversion in the alto, bars 41 and 42 in the bass. These are joined by the continuation of the countersubject,

whose final notes (b′–a sharp′–d″) clearly relate to the coda of the prelude. To this motive falls the task of introducing the entries of the subject and the episodes (bars 12, 15–16, 24–25, 33, 46–47). As in the F Minor Fugue, there is no complete exposition of all four voices after their initial entries. The exposition over, the subject as a whole enters ten more times, but the entries are often so widely separated from one another through episodes that it would do violence to the conception of the form to regard any group as an 'exposition.' Another feature, which we have not previously met in *The Well-Tempered Clavier*, is significant here: namely the anticipation of the entry of the subject by the announcement of its opening notes. For example, after the episode in the soprano, tenor, and bass bars 17–21, the three first notes of the subject (f sharp′–d′–b) appear in the alto voice (bar 19) before the whole subject enters two bars later. A similar case occurs with the tenor b–g–e in bar 28 before the whole subject appears in bar 30. Clearer still is the pre-announcement in bars 34–36[1] and 69–70, where it is extended to the first nine notes of the subject, and extended to voices other than that in which the subject is fully stated. This technique, remarkable in Bach's time, was fashionable in the Italian opera. The singers intoned their aria, broke off and began again only after an episode, and then carried the aria through. The rationale for it was very likely that, with the general inattention in the Italian operatic theater, the beginning of the aria might otherwise be lost (Riemann called this anticipation the 'motto aria,' because in it the beginning was presented in advance like a motto, an apothegm). This practice is to be found even in the church music of that period, whose arias followed closely the

[1] Keller: 44. – Tr.

operatic pattern. In *The Well-Tempered Clavier*, the device succeeds in lending extra significance to the entries of the subject.

As in the F Minor Fugue, Bach uses diatonic episodes in contrast with the dissonant subject. These too have an Italian flavor. The following sequential chain

was a feature of Italian chamber music. Riemann cites, in his *Musikgeschichte in Beispielen* (History of Music in Examples, page 278) an example from a duet for soprano and alto with figured bass by Bach's contemporary Francesco Durante:

which is almost identical with Bach's (the motive moreover is to be found in bars 23–24 of the prelude).

The structure of this fugue is thus as unusual as its subject. Moreover, as in the F Minor Fugue or the *Kyrie* Fugue from the Mass, there is no final climax. Spitta was horrified by its dissonances. He said, it travels 'slowly, sighing, with bitter, even pain-distorted features on a seemingly endless path' and continues: "How little did he count upon the participation of a large musical public who places upon one of his most superior instrumental works [*The Well-Tempered Clavier*] (which was indeed thought of as a whole) such a crown of thorns!" We cannot agree with that any longer. We love the 'precious spices of Bach's dissonances' (Liszt) not only because for us they have long since lost all terror, but because from force and counterforce a rich life answering to a higher law is created; so that with this fugue – as with the *Kyrie* Fugue – we go forth not cast down, but lifted up and strengthened. This fugue is a worthy crown to Bach's great work.

Several prosaic observations need still to be made. In two places Bach felt himself forced to alter the soprano line to avoid c sharp'''.[1] By substituting a c''' sharp in bar 36 on the third-to-last note and in bar 63 on the sixth note the line is corrected. With the tonal answer of the *comes* Bach long debated whether to answer the fifth note of the subject tonally as well as the first (that is, with b instead of c sharp'). He decided in bars 4 and 13 on b (in bar 47[2] on d) because it made the modulation back to the tonic easier. The trill on the penultimate note of the subject may be retained here too as a *pralltrill* to facilitate the listener's recognition of the theme. The significance of the little slurs in the subject, which are original, is obvious; the note of resolution should be played somewhat shorter and weaker. The direction *largo* indicates not so much a specially slow tempo, as solemnity and breadth (Busoni for that reason rewrote the fugue in 4/2 meter). Quarter note equals 48 to 54.

[1] c sharp'' would exceed the compass of Bach's keyboard. – Tr.
[2] Keller says 48 here, but the tonal response on D is in the bass in bar 47. – Tr.

Book II
bwv 870–893

Origin

When in 1723 Bach exchanged his court position at Cöthen for that of cantor and church music director in Leipzig – though initially he felt it would not be entirely proper to become a cantor after being a *Capelmeister* (letter to Erdmann) – the clavier had to take a back seat before the manifold duties of his new position. Nonetheless, from 1730 to 1742 he published the four parts of the *Clavierübung*: the Partitas (BWV 825 to 830), the Italian Concerto, the French Overture (BWV 971/831), Chorale Preludes and Duets (the latter BWV 802–805) and the Goldberg Variations (BWV 988). He returned to preludes and fugues only in his last decade. According to an as yet unverified dating on Schwenke's copy, the second collection of 24 preludes and fugues, later called the *Second Part of The Well-Tempered Clavier*, was completed in 1744. We see Bach in this last period of his life endeavoring to collect earlier works, and create new cyclic works (Musical Offering, BWV 1079; the Art of Fugue, BWV 1080). Thus Book II of *The Well-Tempered Clavier* contains works whose conception ranges over twenty years: some early, and others which must no doubt count as late works.

The London Autograph

For a long time no autograph of *The Well-Tempered Clavier* was known; the editions of Kroll (Peters and Bachgesellschaft) and Bischoff (Steingräber) could be based only on copies. But in 1896 there came to light in the British Museum in London an autograph of Book II which had earlier belonged to Muzio Clementi. After his death it was bequeathed to the Museum by Eliza Wesley, the daughter of the Bach apostle, Samuel Wesley. It consists of loose double pages; the Preludes and Fugues Nos. 4 (C Sharp Minor), 5 (D Major) and 12 (F Minor) are unfortunately lost. Bach neither had these pages bound into a volume nor gave them a collective title.

Through the autograph, many discrepancies of the earlier editions could be clarified, although the copies of Altnikol and

Kirnberger remain valuable because Bach himself made corrections in them.

Style

As it was written over such a long period of time, the second book of *The Well-Tempered Clavier* does not display such stylistic unity as Book I. But for this the greater variety of forms, especially of the preludes, and the high musical content of a number of late pieces make compensation. Since no precise indications are given, an approximate chronological order can only be established through style criticism. Early works (that is, already composed at the time of Book I of *The Well-Tempered Clavier*, or even earlier) are: Numbers 1 (C Major), 3 (C Sharp Major), 4 (only the Fugue), 6 (Prelude), 15 (G Major) and 17 (first part of the Fugue). Indications of a late style (that is, of works conceived between 1735 and 1745) are discernible in: 4 (Prelude), 6 (Fugue), 9 (D Sharp Minor), 12 (F Minor), 13 (F Sharp Major), 14 (F Sharp Minor), 17 (Prelude and second part of the Fugue), 21 (B Flat Major) and 22 (B Flat Minor). With the remaining works, the question must remain undecided; also for the works listed above as having been conceived between 1735 and 1745, the dates are only approximate.

A great deal of specialized research is still needed before firm conclusions about the chronology of Book II can be reached.

The Preludes

The most obvious distinction between Books I and II lies in the greater variety of the preludes. No fewer than ten are in two-part form of which there is only one example (No. 24) in Book I. Three of them (D Major, F Minor, B Flat Major) anticipate the Classic sonata type; three others are two-part inventions (D Sharp Minor, E Minor, A Minor); others (C Minor, E Major, G Major) can be compared to suite movements. Of the remaining fourteen preludes, two are reminiscent of the organ (C Major and G Minor), two are large three-voiced ariosos (C Sharp Minor and F Sharp Minor), four are in Baroque concerto movement form (E Flat Major, F Sharp Major, A Flat Major, B Minor), while the older type is met in the preludes in C Sharp Major (with a joined fughetta) and D Minor.[1]

The Fugues

In Book II there are thirteen three-voice and eleven four-voice fugues; the absence of five-voice and two-voice fugues may be an accident. Here, too, the formal variety is greater than in Book I. Alongside fugues of compact counterpoint (D Major, E Major, F Sharp Minor, A Flat Major, B Flat Minor) stand freer works such as those in F Minor, F Sharp Major, B Flat Major and B Minor. Four fugues are double fugues: C Sharp Minor, A Flat Major, G Sharp Minor and B Major; one (F Sharp Minor) is a triple fugue. In Book II all subjects are answered tonally[2] (with the exception of the G Sharp Minor Fugue); only one (A Minor) modulates to the dominant.

The Connection of Prelude and Fugue

The connection between prelude and fugue is even more difficult to prove in Book II than in Book I. It is demonstrable in the early, later-reworked numbers 1 (C Major), 3 (C Sharp Major), 15 (G Major). Thematic connection exists between the preludes and fugues in C Minor, G Sharp Minor, A Major, A Minor, B Flat Major and B Flat Minor; somewhat weaker also are those in E Flat Major, E Minor, F Minor, F Sharp Minor and G Minor. In several other cases the internal connection is so apparent that a demonstration of the unity of the material is superfluous. It is impossible to generalize on this subject, but rather each case must be treated individually.

Each part of *The Well-Tempered Clavier* has its own character; the second is not the fulfillment of the first, but it is more than a mere collection of scattered works. Each part has traits not found in the other, but only the two together create the whole work, the "48," as the English briefly and concisely designate Books I and II together.

[1] Not mentioned here, but discussed individually later (q.v.) are the preludes in F Major, G Sharp Minor, A Major, B Flat Major and B Flat Minor. – Tr.

[2] There are subjects which beg the question in interesting ways. – Tr.

The Prelude

Bach opened the second part of his work, in contrast to the first, with a festive prelude which reminds us of a *Praeludium pro organo pleno*, and in fact it has close relationships to the Organ Prelude in C Major (BWV 545). As it now stands in *The Well-Tempered Clavier*, it has a rich past behind it. Its earliest form we know through a copy by Kellner (BWV 870a, Prelude 1a), which carries the date '3 July 1726'; however it was probably composed earlier in Bach's first Cöthen years. It numbered only 17 bars (I have included this version in my *Orgelvorspiele alter Meister in allen Tonartem* – Organ Preludes of Old Masters in All the Keys). For *The Well-Tempered Clavier* Bach doubled its size by adding a recapitulation on the subdominant (compare No. 5 in Book I); bars 20–31 correspond to bars 5–16. Like the cited organ prelude, it is introduced by three bars on a tonic organ-point and closed similarly. This second version (BWV 870b, Prelude 1b), which is in Bach's autograph, was fundamentally reworked once again so that in many places the figuration – as in the C Sharp Major Fugue in Book II – was altered to thirty-second notes. The version of the prelude generally played today (BWV 870, Prelude 1) came down to us through Altnikol's copy, though the simpler version of the autograph can hold its own next to it. In my *Urtext* edition of the second volume of *The Well-Tempered Clavier* (Peters Edition No. 4691b) I have therefore included both versions as well as, for the first time, in the appendix, a version of bars 15–19 later rejected by Bach. The technique of the prelude is that of a *Toccata di durezze e ligature*, an improvisation consisting of an interlaced series of harmonies. Bach sets the harmonic texture in motion through a division of the part-writing in which all the voices take part in such a way that no part is independent as in a fugue or in an organ movement: in several places (bars 5, 8, 20, 22) the tenor transfers unexpectedly into the bass; the individual voices are parts of a predominantly harmonic texture. This prelude seems to contrast irreconcilably with the fugue; but despite the entirely different mood, the exquisite workmanship of the fugue makes it a worthy companion to the prelude.

The performance requires dignity and breadth. Quarter note equals 54 to 58.

The Fugue à 3

In its earliest form, this fugue came down to us through Kellner as a *fughetta* (BWV 8701a) together with the prelude (BWV 870a, Prelude 1a). It was in c time and ended after measure 33 (which equals measure 67 in the later version). Bach rewrote it in 2/4 time thus doubling the metric accents (compare the reverse case in No. 24 of Book II) and giving the fugue a greater inner liveliness. He further added a coda of sixteen bars (bars 68–83).

The subject derives its special character from the mordent, written out in bar 1, sharply accenting the top of the melody in bar 2, and gradually losing itself in the rolling sixteenths. These latter form the only counterpoint to the subject, and together they make up the entire fugue. Its structure is remarkably symmetrical: four main sections with expositions of the subject separated by three episodes. The plan is as follows: exposition, bars 1–13; first episode (with the subject in the upper voices, the countersubject in the bass) bars 13–22; as early as bar 21[1] the alto enters with the second exposition, the soprano follows in bar 25, the bass dropping out; second episode, bars 29–39; third exposition, bars 39–55 (bass bar 39, alto bar 47, soprano bar 51); third episode, analogous to the first, bars 55–68;[2] fourth exposition bars 68–83 (bass bar 68, alto bar 72, soprano bar 76). Thus we admire in this fugue above all the mastery of its formal plan notwithstanding its high spirits which intensify increasingly toward the close. In the coda the subject flows as if submerged, but lifts itself in the soprano entry to a triumphant breadth (Wanda Landowska likens this to the sight

[1] Keller: 20. – Tr.
[2] Keller: 58. – Tr.

of a high-rearing horse, and warns against closing the fugue with a *ritardando*). In the first version of the fugue, after Kellner, there are fingerings which Bach may have himself written in during a lesson. (They are printed in the *Ausgabe* edition of the Bach *Gesellschaft* **XXXVI**, page 224, and show that the fifth finger should be avoided as far as possible, especially in the left hand; in the downward scale passages of the right hand, the little finger is bent under the third finger.)

Performance: in order to unify the fugue with the prelude, take the tempo of the fugue exactly twice as fast. It should not be thought of as too light and dance-like but rather be performed with a certain masculine humor; the chief sections and the episodes should be clearly set off one against the other. Quarter note equals 108 to 116.

BOOK II: NO. 2 IN C MINOR, BWV 871

The Prelude

This prelude can be interpreted in two different ways: either as a dance movement or as a two-part invention. As a dance movement it resembles the *allemandes* in the Bach suites in having two repeated sections of 12 plus 16 bars (compare the *allemande* of the Sixth French Suite, BWV 817), although the characteristic sixteenth-note upbeat is missing. Also, as in the majority of suite movements, the structure of the whole is regular except for occasional details. Thus, the first part of the prelude consists of $4+4\frac{1}{2}+3\frac{1}{2}=12$ bars; the second, of $4+5+4+3=16$ bars. In the technique of its structure, this prelude is a two-part invention. Its double subject (the rolling sixteenth notes and the skipping eighth notes) is inverted in the second bar, developed further in bars 3 and 4, and sequences then lead to a close in E flat major. The second part varies and extends the first.

The prelude is closely connected to the fugue. If one reduces the sixteenth notes to eighth notes in both movements,

this is made immediately plain. Moreover, both are in two sections and have the same number of bars (28).

In order to emphasize this connection, and to guard the prelude against an *étude*-like performance, one should not play it too fast, but with quiet, somewhat thoughtful delicacy. Quarter note equals 76 to 84.

The Fugue à 4

The straightforward, unpretentious subject seems to reach back to the style of the pre-Bach masters and to possess little individuality; in its simplicity, however, it has an inner strength which anticipates the Art of Fugue (BWV 1080). For a long time the fugue remains three-voiced, the lowest voice being sometimes handled as bass, sometimes as tenor. Only in bar 19 does the true bass enter with the subject in augmentation to make the texture four-voiced. This reservation of the bass for a late entry of increased significance makes this fugue resemble the great Organ Fugue in C Major (BWV 546), which remains four-voiced for a long time until the bass enters with the subject in augmentation and raises it to an unimaginable climax. In more modest fashion we see the same thing here. In its first part (bars 1–14) the thematic work is so concentrated that there is no room for a special countersubject. The subject begins to be transformed in the rising line of the bass (bar 5) and the countermotion of the soprano (bar 6):

In bar 7, too, we hear allusions to the subject in the alto.

In bars 8 and 9 the leading of the subject is taken away from the bass and transferred to the soprano; but all this is presented only as a prelude to the second part, which begins with an old-fashioned triple stretto: the subject in the soprano is counterpointed with its augmentation in the alto and its inversion in the tenor (bars 14–16).

From here on, stretti never cease: in bars 16–17 alto, soprano, and tenor are strettoed, in bars 17–18 the soprano (third-last note of bar 17) with the alto (later copyists have sought to ease the harmonic harshness at this point by substituting a flat′ and d flat″ for a′ and d″ in the tenor and soprano in bar 18). Only now does the bass enter, as though on the pedals of an organ, in long notes, and adds immediately two entries of the subject in inversion and in direct motion (bars 21 and 22) which bring the fugue to a close in the middle of bar 23. But Bach finds it impossible to stop here. He adds a coda with stretti, first of alto and soprano at two eighth notes' distance, then of soprano (the last eighth note of bar 24) and alto (second eighth note in bar 25), then of bass and alto simultaneously (bar 26), and confirms it all with an unfugal, striking close in the minor key! In this way the second part of this fugue grows to a dimension which the first part did not hint at.

Performance: legato (no caesura in the subject), severe, reflective. Quarter note equals 58 to 63.

BOOK II: NO. 3 IN C SHARP MAJOR, BWV 872

Both pieces derive from earlier works and were perhaps written before Book I of *The Well-Tempered Clavier*. For inclusion in Book II, they were extensively re-worked.

The Prelude

The earliest form of this prelude (BWV 872a, Prelude 3a) is
found in a copy by Kellner, where it is in C major, and the
harmonies, as in the introduction to the A Minor Fugue (BWV
944) and the arpeggios in the Chromatic Fantasy (BWV 903),
are only sketched:

Bach transposed it to C sharp major and worked out the broken
chords into a four-voiced texture whose rhythmic diversity one
cannot fail to admire: the bass moves in quiet quarter notes
punctuated with rests, the tenor in repeated eighth notes, while
the alto and the soprano are interlinked in sixteenth-note
motives. This elaboration follows the earlier sketch exactly
except for bar 22 where the figuration should read:

(Bach's version is either a writing error or maybe he wished to
avoid the troublesome notation.)

A *fughetta* in 3/8 time follows the preamble. We have here a
parallel with the E Flat Major Prelude in Book I: neither piece
requires the addition of a further fugue.

In its rewriting the *fughetta* was improved in details. For
example, the chromatic leading of the alto in bars 44–46 is still
missing in the first version, likewise the small suspensions. It is
labelled *allegro* (the prelude is thus a quiet *andante*) – *allegro*, not
vivace. The prelude must be bathed in euphony with a *crescendo*
in the last bars leading to the *forte* of the *fughetta*. Quarter note
equals 76; *fughetta*, eighth note equals 152.

The Fugue à 3

In its first version this fugue was also in C major and numbered only nineteen bars (BWV 872a, *Fughetta* 3a). Bach expanded it for *The Well-Tempered Clavier* but in a different manner from his reworking of the fugues in C Major, E Minor and A Flat Major. Instead of composing a supplement or second part to it, he subdivided it into its sections and enlarged these. In the original the change into minor in bars 14–16, the augmentation of the subject and a second shift to the minor in bars 25–30: all were missing. But who can see the joints in the new fugue? As in the C Major Prelude in Book II, Bach later refined the details of his new version further through the insertion of thirty-second notes (in bars 16–27). But one thing remains a puzzle for us. Where does the subject end? Several editions (for example, Brandt-Buys) limit it to the first four notes, Riemann to the first six, others (Tovey, David) want to stretch it to the twelfth note (f sharp). It is remarkable that no one has chosen the most obvious limit, namely the eighth note (c sharp). Granted that Bach works in the second half of the fugue almost exclusively with the first four notes, but one must not therefore assume that this insignificant motive could carry the entire fugue. The exposition, too, which at once introduces stretto and inversion, is curious; even more strange are the many short-breathed cadences, which divide the first part (until bar 14) into many little sections. Only from this point does the fugue begin to bloom, and in the second half, for the most part entirely newly composed, can the voices finally sing out.

Toward the close the fugue grows in both outward and inward intensity; its close on the third leaves us enriched in a way which the first part of the fugue did not let us suspect. This expansion is also prepared by the two augmentations of the first four notes of the subject in bars 25 (alto) and 27 (bass); the diminutions (bars 5, 6, 18, 19, 33 and 34) stem from the first version of the fugue.

This fugue has given rise to very varied interpretations. Many conceive it pompously, gravely, others almost as a *scherzo*.

Especially in its newly composed parts, however, it continues
the mood of the prelude; it also is bathed in euphony. The
eighth notes followed by rests in the subject are really detached
quarter notes, and they ought to be held somewhat longer than
written. If one plays them with their exact value, one hears in
certain places a false voice leading (for example in bar 2:
c sharp″–g sharp′–b′–g sharp′). Quarter note equals 63 to 69.

BOOK II: NO. 4 IN C SHARP MINOR, BWV 873

Bach here treats this key differently from Book I. This prelude
is one of the most fine-grained in the entire *Well-Tempered Clavier*.
It was only later linked to the fugue, which was probably composed earlier in Cöthen, originally in C minor. Prelude and
fugue are only conventionally related.

The Prelude

This prelude could be regarded as a contribution of the aging
Bach to the *empfindsam* style; it is more aristocratic than the
F Minor Prelude in Book II and in Bach's work there is only
one counterpart: the third movement of the Trio Sonata from
the Musical Offering (BWV 1079). That the autograph has been
lost must be especially regretted because the numerous, important ornaments vary in Altnikol and Kirnberger's manuscripts. One can imagine the three-voiced texture being played
by a string trio or by three woodwinds – among the keyboard
instruments the clavichord is the most nearly suitable. But how
much passion is hidden within it; not sentimentality, but true
sentiment! Bach would not be Bach if he had not confined it to
a strict form and, in so doing, objectified it. The outline is in
five sections:

Main section: bars 1–26 (17+9 bars)
Subsidiary section: bars 27–32

Main section: bars 33–49 (6+11 bars)
Subsidiary section: bars 50–56
Main section: bars 56–62

What Richard Wagner said of another prelude of *The Well-Tempered Clavier*: 'The endless melody here was already pre-formed,' would apply without limitation to the C Sharp Minor Prelude, whose three voices so interpenetrate one another that they create one great melody whose first caesura lies at the beginning of bar 17. The motives are transformed constantly. The motive

becomes

(bar 5) and

(bar 17). The rising triad of the episode (bar 27[1]) stems from the beginning of the bass (bar 1): also the bass leading in bars 9 to 12 is a transformation of the f sharp″–g sharp″–e″ in bar 4; and so on. The ornaments, in Kirnberger sometimes little notes, sometimes little crosses, are fully written out in Altnikol and 'thereby cloud the harmony' as Scheibe reproached Bach (see page 43).

Performance: most subtly expressive in all three voices; quiet quarter notes. Dotted quarter note equals 48.

The Fugue à 3

This fugue, as we know from a copy by Kellner, was originally in C minor. For inclusion in *The Well-Tempered Clavier* it was transcribed into C sharp minor, but otherwise taken over un-

[1] Keller: 37. – Tr.

altered. Bach apparently had no fugue worthy of the prelude, and therefore reached back to this older work. Subjects which move in uninterrupted, equal rhythmic units were frequent in earlier literature; with Bach himself they appear principally among the youthful works (the final fugues to the toccatas, two fugues in A minor BWV 944 and 894, the latter also in 12/16 meter); in *The Well-Tempered Clavier* this type occurs only twice more, in the E Minor Fugue in Book I and the G Major Fugue in Book II. Subjects of this sort easily lead the composer to a superfluity of sequence building, which is also a characteristic of this C Sharp Minor Fugue.

It is the first double fugue in *The Well-Tempered Clavier* which develops both themes first individually, then together. The second subject, which enters in bar 35, has however no significance on its own,

but is immediately counterpointed with the first in stretto, so that one may question whether this fugue is really a double fugue. The independence of the second subject is further lessened by the fact that it has already appeared in bar 27 in smaller note values, and by its having foreshadowed in the bass in bars 17–19, and in the soprano bars 20–22. This is therefore a border-line case. Sequences taken from the subject serve as episodes; a significant countersubject does not appear. The first exposition is followed by a second exposition of soprano (bar 16), alto (bar 17) and bass (bar 20). In the third exposition, the subject is inverted; the soprano enters in bar 24, the alto follows it in bar 26, the bass in bar 28; the alto contributes an additional entrance in bar 30 in the tenor range. In the fourth exposition the second subject enters in the soprano in bar 35, bar 36 in the alto, bar 38 (with upbeat) in the bass. In the fifth and last exposition, both subjects are linked together: 1 plus 2 in soprano and bass at the lower fifth in bar 48, 2 plus 1 in soprano and bass at the octave in bar 55, 1 plus 2 in alto and bass at the fifth below in bar 61, 2 plus 1 at the fourth below in the soprano and alto in bar 66, in addition to 2 plus 1, shifted a half bar in alto and bass in bars 67–68! The C Sharp Minor version deviates in three details from the one in C Minor. In all three cases the original version is the better, and maybe was not adopted solely through a copying error: in bar 26 the alto read:

the bass in bar 41:

And in the next to last measure of the bass:

(on the whole this fugue sounds more natural and more convincing in C minor than in C sharp minor). Dotted eighth note equals 116.

BOOK II: NO. 5 IN D MAJOR, BWV 874

The Prelude

This prelude radiates the brilliance of its key and is given festal instrumentation: a fiery fanfare of the trumpets, to which the woodwinds (flutes and oboes) answer; in bar 5 the strings join in with energetic bow-strokes and complete the orchestra of a Bach *Overture*. It is no prelude, but rather a fully formed sonata movement with exposition, development and recapitulation. In its structure, it excels many youthful works of Haydn and Mozart. The regularity of the form also places it close to the Viennese classics: the exposition numbers 16 bars of which 4 are taken up with the statement of the subject, 8 by its elaboration, 4 by the closing section. The development contains 24 bars ($4 \times 4 + 8$ bars leading back from B minor); the recapitulation with its 16 bars follows the exposition exactly (naturally without the modulation to the dominant). Only the second subject is missing from the sonata form of the high Classic period, but Bach's music is still the *'musique d'une teneur'* [music of one character or *Affekt*]. These very modern traits are in contrast with the constant three-voiced texture of an older style (but the structure is so rich that one is hardly aware of this limitation), and with the old-fashioned inversion of the theme at the beginning of the second part (which caused Riemann to describe the prelude as a gigue). The double time signature ¢ 12/8 signifies a lively tempo and a duplet performance of the eighth notes in bars 2 and 4 (which may be adjusted to the triplet rhythm in bar 18). The dottings indicate triplets as in the E Minor Fugue in Book II; at the close of the second part, the mordents should be added by analogy with those of the first part. If one follows the fanfare of bars 1 and 3 with the duplets *piano*, the continuation should be *mezzo forte*; the last four bars, after the model of several sonatas of Corelli, can be played *piano*. In bar 36 the reading in Kirnberger's version (the autograph is lost)

represents a timid weakening of Altnikol's version:

The overflowing joy of life of the prelude (with, according to Busoni, an admixture of comfort) demands a fiery performance and a rich articulation. Dotted quarter note equals 84.

The Fugue à 4

The prelude is to this fugue as the festive orchestral introduction of a cantata is to the choral fugue which follows (e.g., the *Ratswahlkantate* – BWV 29 [Cantata for the Inauguration of the

Council, *Wir danken dir, Gott, wir danken dir*] in the same key). Hence, the present fugue makes its appearance with seeming modesty and is in danger of being undervalued. Busoni made this mistake when he suggested that it is 'a choral fugue in the conventional style of Catholic church music, perhaps on the text *Christe Eleison.*' At first glance, the music of this fugue appears to confirm that judgment; but anyone who looks at it more closely and observes its masterly structure will ask himself, what Catholic church composer of the eighteenth century could have written such a fugue? In certain respects Busoni is undoubtedly right: it is not a typical clavier fugue, and since the motive (b) of the subject is heard ceaselessly, almost a hundred times, in every possible kind of stretto, there is a real danger of thematic and rhythmic monotony. This Bach overcomes through an incessant growth of the contrapuntal art. The formal structure is binary (bars 1–27 and 27–50[1]); as in the fugues in E Flat Minor and A Minor in Book I, the intensification of the fugal technique is symmetrically arranged. The exposition (bars 1–10) is followed by two entries in the alto (bar 10) and soprano (bar 11), then of both voices in stretto (bar 14). After an episode of four and one half bars (bars 16–20) with (b), the tenor (bar 21), soprano (bar 22) and alto (bar 22) enter in minor in stretto and close the first part in bar 27 in F sharp minor.[2] Now at a distance of two eighth notes, bass, soprano and alto enter in stretto at the octave; here the alto could perhaps be completed thus:

The next stretto combines tenor, alto and soprano at the sixth (bars 33–34). Another episode with (b) follows; the voices enter widely separated from one another in order to make room for the tenor, which enters in bar 40 with a welcome interruption of the continuous stretti of (b), whereupon the last exposition crowns all with a stretto at the third below of all four voices from the top to the bottom at the distance of two eighth notes:

[1] Keller: 51. – Tr.
[2] Keller omits mention of an obvious bass entry in bar 25. – Tr.

This writing is comparable to the close of the B Flat Minor Fugue of Book I, and, on a keyboard instrument, just as unplayable.

The high praise we paid to the fugue at the beginning may thus have to be somewhat modified: as a fugue in pure vocal style it cannot match the Fugue in E Major in Book II, as a stretto fugue it cannot match the E Flat Minor Fugue in Book I and the B Flat Minor in Book II.

Performance: the player can make no greater error than to split the subject through phrasing into (a) and (b). Further, in the many (indeed too many) stretti of (b) the longer lines should not be dismembered. One should guard against an excessively flowing tempo which would weaken the seriousness in which this fugue must be approached (a mood perhaps more easily realized if one imagines it in 4/2 time). Quarter note equals 83 (like the prelude).

BOOK II: NO. 6 IN D MINOR, BWV 875

The Prelude

This prelude, built on passage work and broken harmonies, is a youthful work whose first version (BWV 875a, Preamble 6a) like those of numbers 1, 3 and 4, survives in a copy by Kellner. After its reworking it looks, in the second part of *The Well-*

Tempered Clavier, like a stripling among mature men. As with the C Sharp Major Fugue, Bach expanded it through insertions:

in place of bars 5–17, there were originally only two measures (i.e. the exchange of voices in bars 5–8 and the ensuing contrary movement of the two hands had not yet been discovered);

bars 30–33 (as a comparable exchange of voices of bars 26–29) were also missing;

bars 37–38 were inserted, and in several places the figuration was enriched, for example in bars 47–49 (=bars 30–32 of the original version):

Although the structure is only two-voiced throughout, how full and rich it sounds, its aggressive character sharpened further through mordents! Especially bold, but logical and convincing, is the collision of b flat' and b natural in bar 37. The crossing of the hands in bars 18–25 and 57–61 is most comfortably performed on a harpsichord with the two manuals. The missing mordent should be added in bar 42.

Performance: lively, with tense energy, sharply articulated. Quarter note equals 112.

The Fugue à 3

The stormy movement of its prelude is taken up by this fugue, whose subject transforms the fall from octave to tonic of the prelude's subject into a passionate ascent. The prelude is an early work; the fugue must stem from Bach's most mature period. The *ductus* of its subject has a relationship not only with the fugue of the Dorian Toccata (BWV 538) but also with the subject of the Musical Offering (BWV 1079); its taut triplets also have an affinity with the C Minor Fantasy (BWV 906). And how richly equipped it is! Already in the subject itself two contrary forces are at work: the charging triplets are opposed by a measured, chromatically falling eighth-note movement. Added to this is a countersubject, which struggles against that fall.

This is material enough for a fugue in the grand style, e.g., that of the Dorian Toccata. But this does not happen. The rich material is not entirely utilized, and this fugue with its 27 bars makes a fragmentary impression. Further, it scarcely leaves its key, the beginning of the modulation towards F major (bars 8–9) is deflected back again, and after the first exposition there is no complete re-exposition. Instead there are two effective stretti at the distance of a quarter note: bars 14–15 between the alto and soprano, bars 17–18 in the inversion between the alto and bass; and there is a final climax, beginning in the depths with an impulse worthy of Beethoven! Thus, even if it has not made use of all the possibilities inherent in its material, this fugue is indeed a short work of great forcefulness and terseness. With the similarly short prelude it creates an ideal unity.

In the autograph copy, the soprano in bars 13–14 originally read:

a reading which several copies and editions followed; Bach however erased this place and led into the next entry of the subject with animation from above through octave transposition:

Performance: with controlled energy, elastically resilient, with a clear caesura in the subject after the fifth eighth note. Quarter note equals 69 to 80.

BOOK II: NO. 7 IN E FLAT MAJOR, BWV 876

The Prelude

Again a new type, not previously encountered in *The Well-Tempered Clavier*, greets us here: a prelude which, in its innocence and charm, could have been written for lute or theorbo. It has a certain similarity with the lute prelude in E Flat Major ascribed to Bach (BWV 998). It also shows inner affinity to the tenor aria, '*Seht, was die Liebe tut*' from the Cantata BWV 85.

Thus it is no "*merry gigue*" (Riemann) but rather a subjective little private curio, which best fits the clavichord. Its structure falls in five sections like that of the C Sharp Minor Prelude in Book II. The chief sections are: bars 1–20, 32–46, and 57–71; subsidiary sections (in minor): bars 21–32 and 47–56. The transitions are fluent; Bach's art of developing one section from another is here clearly displayed. Busoni suggested exchanging the E Flat Major Preludes from Book I and Book II (see page 73). That would in each case give prelude and fugue a similarity of sound, but the charm of the contrast through which both grow together to a higher unity, especially in Book II, would then be missing.

Theoretically, the suspension in bars 2, 4 and 62 should have the length of two eighth notes. But that would create ugly parallel fourths with the bass. With a duration of only an eighth note the suspension fits better into the prevailing motion (compare especially bars 37–44) than it would if extended to a dotted quarter note. In bar 3[1] the third note of the bass in the autograph copy reads B flat; with Kirnberger, however, d, which represents an improvement. In the last quarter of bar 49 the augmented fourth c' to f sharp' (Kirnberger) is better than the diminished fifth c'' to f sharp' with Altnikol.[2] Bars 52 and 54 show how precisely Bach notated. Here, and only here, the bass note has a quarter note because in the upper voice there is a suspension.

Performance: gently flowing, with delicate expression. Dotted quarter note equals 76.

The Fugue à 4

Riemann set the following text to the subject: '*Lob, Preis und Dank sei dem Herrn, der uns erlöst von dem Tod*' (Honor, praise and thanks be to the Lord, who has released us from death) and in so doing he has strikingly characterized this fugue. The words, like their musical setting, might form the material of a motet by Michael Haydn. The strengths and weaknesses of this fugue are thereby equally indicated. Its strengths: that it has a singable, easily remembered subject, and is readily understood in its elaborateness even by a layman; its weaknesses: that it 'already in the subject distills the smell of double counterpoint,' as van Bruyck wickedly expressed it, and that its sequences in the stereotyped rhythm ♩♩♩|♩♩♩♩♩|♩♩♩| are used almost excessively. But how great is its euphony, how lively its flow! Its structure is individual. The exposition is followed by only one re-exposition, in which first tenor and bass (bars 30–31)

---

[1] Keller says here bar 5; this is obviously a misprint. – Tr.

[2] The translator here finds himself disagreeing with Keller: the higher C, Altnikol's version, seems to grow more logically from the context and to be resolved on the B flat in the measure following. – Tr.

enter together in stretto, then alto and soprano (bars 37–38);
a third stretto of bass and soprano (bars 59–60) ends this, the
most easily understood of all the fugues in *The Well-Tempered
Clavier*.[1]

In performance one should beware of too rigid and military
a conception, which the subject too readily suggests. This fugue
must be saturated with euphony, like a choral fugue. The ¢
sign signifies not an especially fast tempo, but rather char-
acterizes its *a capella* style. Half note equals 76 (like the prelude).

BOOK II: NO. 8 IN D SHARP MINOR, BWV 877

The Prelude

This prelude and fugue are in the rarest and most uncom-
fortable of all keys. Several editions have for that reason rewritten
them into E flat minor; it is most probable that – as in the case
of the D Sharp Minor Fugue in Book I – the original tonality
was D minor. If one plays both of them in this, to us, familiar
tonality, they sound so very natural that there can scarcely be
any doubt about the original conception.

The prelude is a two-part invention of 16 plus 20 bars with
both parts repeated, the reprise in the second part abbreviated in
the manner of a pre-Classic sonata movement. The two-part
invention in E Major (BWV 777) could serve as a model for it;
in Book II of *The Well-Tempered Clavier* this type is encountered
once more, in the Prelude in E Minor. The structure is familiar
from many examples: a two-bar subject, put together from (a)
and (b), is stated, answered in the lower voice, and elaborated
with half-bar sequences (in which the derivation from bar 2
should not be overlooked).

---

[1] Keller fails to mention an entry of the subject in the tenor in bar 53. – Tr.

Then the play repeats in the relative major key F sharp; the close in the dominant (A sharp minor) is enriched with thirty-second notes in the same way as the C Major Prelude and the C Sharp Major Fugue in their later forms. In the development-like middle section, this figuration is combined with the main motive; the sequences, with which the recapitulation is prepared (bars 25–27), correspond to those of bars 6–8. In the recapitulation, the lower voice begins (bar 28), the upper voice follows it a measure later.

It is a 'matter of fact' prelude which should be played objectively, clearly and neutrally in expression, one to which a medium tempo is appropriate, perhaps quarter note equals 72.

The Fugue à 4

This fugue carries with it a heavy burden of thought. Its subject after thrice repeating the tonic, lifts itself in three laborious steps to the fifth (as in the F Sharp Minor Fugue in Book I and the B Flat Minor Fugue in Book II) and sinks again back to the tonic note. Consequently, the fugue is dominated by great seriousness, beginning with the subject, further intensified by the fact that virtually nowhere do rests relax its compact structure. Its form equally renounces any relaxation through episodes. The latter are limited to the barest necessary transitions, so that one subject entry follows the other. The subject is everything, the countersubject, which ponderously intrudes itself upon the subject

(it is taken from the motive c ×'–d♯'–e♯' of the subject) is soon abandoned. The second exposition follows immediately after the first (bar 15 in the bass, bar 17 in the alto, bar 19 in the tenor, bar 21 in the soprano); to this follows at once the third (alto bar 23 with three upbeat eighth notes, bass bar 25, soprano bar 27 [in C sharp minor!]). The fourth and last exposition is widely stretched out: the alto enters in bar 30 (in B major), the tenor in bar 32 (on D sharp),[1] finally, after a broad intensification, with motives derived from the subject,

the bass (bar 41 with upbeat). Here, through the chords which impressively accompany the subject, the texture finally receives light and air, whereupon a final entry of the soprano (bar 44 with upbeat), mirrored in the tenor, closes the fugue. The somewhat colorless reflective character of the prelude is deepened and darkened in the fugue to a heavy melancholy, from which even the major cadence cannot offer escape. The performer, who must battle with all this and with the tonality besides, can scarcely present the fugue satisfactorily on a keyboard instrument; is that perhaps the reason why it is played so rarely, despite its merit? Quarter note equals 56 to 60.

BOOK II: NO. 9 IN E MAJOR, BWV 878

The Prelude

From the shadow of the D Sharp Minor Fugue we step, in the E Major Prelude, into the brightness and warmth of a summer landscape. It is a *pastorale* in the form of a large suite movement. Its regular structure, built from four-bar groups, made yet more charming through several small deviations, corresponds to such a suite movement. Thus the first part consists of $4+4+4+5+3+4=24$ bars,[2] the second of $4+3+5+4+5+5+4=30$ bars.

---

[1] Keller says here 'in D sharp minor,' but the key is ambiguous at this point. – Tr.

[2] Keller omits one four-bar group in his original here. – Tr.

Here we must especially admire how Bach succeeds in developing an entire movement from an unpretentious motive of only two notes. From

and

Both motives are begun by the soprano, taken up by the alto, then extended in the soprano and imitated by the bass. The first four-bar groups consist of just this. The second repeats the play on the dominant, with an exchanged entry of the voices; then the motive is broadened over two measures, and transfers from the soprano to the bass (bars 11–12). In the next five-bar group the subject runs through all three voices and leads to the closing group, whose organpoint, divided into eighth notes, corresponds to that of the beginning. The eighth notes ring out like bell tones, transfer into the upper voice, and lead to a close on the third in the dominant. The second half of the prelude turns toward the minor and manages to deal more freely with the thematic material of the first part. Here there are, in the fifth bar before the end, four different readings in the bass:

The first is that of the autograph copy, the second that of Altnikol, the third Kirnberger, the fourth in later copies – let each one choose for himself! This prelude is, without detriment to its own exceptional merit, truly a prelude to its fugue, with which it is also thematically connected. If one considers the *comes* of the fugue (bars 2–3),[1] its first two notes are exactly the same as the beginning of the prelude; its continuation (e′–d sharp′–c sharp′–b) is contained in bar 2 of the prelude.

Performance: quietly flowing, in the style of a *pastorale.* Quarter note equals 60.

[1] Keller: 3. – Tr.

The Fugue à 4

Of all Bach's fugues in vocal style, this one is nearest to the style of Palestrina. It has a purity and beauty reminiscent of Raphael. Its subject does not show characteristics of Bach, but goes back to old traditions. In Kirnberger's copy there is a statement that it stems from J. K. F. Fischer's *Ariadne musica*:

The subject had however already appeared in a Froberger *Ricercare* in the phrygian mode

and is actually a musical archetype, underlying also the melody of *L'homme armé*, appearing in the *Gradus ad Parnassum* of Fux, and providing the subject of the finale of Mozart's Jupiter Symphony (KV 551).

Upon this old classic theme Bach has written a fugue in the old classic form, viz. a motet. The subject has been supplied with an obbligato countersubject similarly adapted to the requirements of strict counterpoint:

To the exposition in the order bass, tenor, alto, soprano (bars 1–9) follows as a second exposition a stretto of alto and tenor at half a bar's distance, and of bass and soprano at a similar distance. This is continued by the countersubject and led toward C sharp minor (bars 9–16). In the third exposition (bars 16–24) the subject is chromatically accompanied, and strettoed at the distance of a whole bar: between alto and soprano bars 16–17, between bass and tenor bars 19–20. The fourth exposi-

tion (F sharp minor) provides the subject with passing notes
and brings it in stretto between soprano and alto:

and then (bar 25) between bass and tenor (both are difficult to
hear). The end of this exposition is concealed by the entry
on the fifth, in which the subject is diminished to half value:

(entrances: soprano, alto, tenor, bass): it closes in G sharp
minor (bar 35) and gives way to the last exposition in which
the three lower voices link the subject together as in bars 9–10,
while above them the countersubject leads into the heights, and
introduces the last soprano entry in the highest position, reserved
until that point. From this luminous height the three voices flow
weightlessly downwards; the bass enters with the subject for the
last time, the soprano accompanies its downward movement,
and the fugue closes with a subjective turn which brings us back
again to earth.

No instrument can reproduce the transfigured beauty of this
movement, unique among Bach's whole life's work. What
remains is an earthly fragment which the fantasy of the player
must conquer. Half note equals 60 (like the prelude).

BOOK II: NO. 10 IN E MINOR, BWV 879

The Prelude

This two-part and two-voiced prelude is, in character, a *Corrente*
(the Italian version of the *Courante*): in its structure and its
thematic development, it is a great two-part invention like the
D Sharp Minor Prelude which is closely related to it. Its two
parts consist of 48 plus 60 (60 = 24 + 36) small-sized bars joined

together regularly; bars 81–108 are a reprise of bars 24–48, expanded through a coda. For the subject itself perhaps 6/8 meter would have been more suitable; evidently Bach preferred the more manageable 3/8 meter because of the many compartmentalizations of the motive. On first acquaintance, this piece makes a somewhat indifferent and brittle impression; when one studies it, however, it takes on increasingly more life and a special coloration which might bring to mind a line of Hugo von Hofmannsthal: '*Es läuft der Frühlingswind durch kahle Alleen*' (The spring wind blows through leafless passageways). Yet our attention is first drawn to the structure of this model invention, in which the running motive of the first two bars supplies absolutely everything. That motive is always there, it is transposed, elaborated, turned upside down in the second part, strettoed (bars 24–28) and combined with the expanded leap from bars 3–4:

This all happens so naturally and in such an unforced manner that one is scarcely aware of the art that produces this superb work. In bars 3, 4, 12 and 22, there are sixteenth notes in the autograph; the thirty-second notes are found only in copies.

The prelude has a close connection with the fugue. Its flow, its flexible turns are confirmed in the masculine and determined entrance of the fugue subject with its rolling triplet movement. The contours of the fugue subject are already suggested in the *ductus* of the prelude:

Performance: with inner liveliness and humor, with caesuras after the first sixteenth note in the soprano in bars 7, 9, 15, 24, 26, 28 and 45, and in the bass in bars, 11, 17, 19, 21, 24, 25, 27 and 37; correspondingly in the second part. Dotted quarter note equals 60.

The Fugue à 3

What a contrast between this and the preceding fugue! There a subject of quiet, pure beauty from which Bach built one of his most ingenious fugues; here a subject laden with energy, starting impatiently, pressing forward, rhythmically varied, ending in rolling triplets, the longest in the entire work – but from the point of view of compositional technique a subject from whose riches one of the most simple fugues of *The Well-Tempered Clavier* emerges. It owes its life to the drive of its subject and the countersubject allotted to it, and foregoes all compositional devices whatever. It is a brilliant fugue for the performer; its counterpart in the first book is the G Major Fugue; but Brandt-Buys rightly remarks that it 'is fed from deeper springs than the life-loving humor of the G Major Fugue.'

The countersubject, which rises to the octave

serves, in its second half, to stabilize the texture. Bach handles it – like the entire work – very freely; for example, he distributes it in bars 13–18 between the soprano and alto.

After the exposition, the subject enters only six more times, namely, in three groups of two which one could consider incomplete re-expositions, but which rather give the impression of being quotations from the subject based on improvisation: each with upbeat in bars 24 and 30, soprano and alto (G major–D major); in bars 42 and 50, bass and alto (B minor–E minor); in bars 60 and 72, soprano and bass (A minor–E minor). The final entry was added only later; in the autograph the fugue ends after bar 70:

Bach must have felt that the forces he had unleashed had not been brought sufficiently under control, so after a half-cadence with a fermata, he added a further sixteen bars. The movement comes to a standstill a second time on a fermata in bar 83 before the final four bars at last bring it to a definite close. Beneath the fermata on d sharp″ there is an *adagio* in Kirnberger's copy; this means that it should be prepared through a *ritardando*. The jagged fall of the bass in bar 81

has a true pedal effect, and also the entry of the soprano in the following bar calls to mind a famous organ work of Bach, the close of the A Minor Prelude (BWV 543). The staccato signs in the subject are dots in the autograph, wedges with Kirnberger. The dotted eighth notes are obviously to be performed as triplets. In bar 83 the chord beneath the fermata in the autograph reads A–f sharp–b, with Kirnberger, however, c–f sharp–a. The first version is in most editions; Kroll has taken over the second, the more dissonant and the more interesting, perhaps a subsequent correction by Bach.

The performance requires a powerfully controlled *allegro*. Half note equals 69.

BOOK II: NO. 11 IN F MAJOR, BWV 880

The Prelude

This great, significant prelude has a form which is not found again in *The Well-Tempered Clavier*: it consists of four sections of 16 + 16 + 24 + 16 bars with the modulatory cycle of F major–C major–A minor–D minor–F major. The fourth section is a recapitulation of the first, although there can be no question here of a tendency toward sonata form; rather have we here a concerto movement in which the subsidiary sections have been omitted. The structure is five-voiced, but the polyphony is not entirely strict; it thins out into three- or four-part writing as comfortable playability requires. Everything breathes rest and peace. The eighth notes circumscribe a harmonic texture which might perhaps sound like this without decorations:

in quarter-note movement thus:

On this background, surrounded by legato slurs which Bach himself indicated for the first bars, lie protectively the eighth notes, which transfer from voice to voice. The metric structure of the four sections is harmonious and without conflicts. The first section consists of four four-bar groups; likewise the second; the third has a longer breath with $8+8+8=24$ bars. Where dissonances enter, they are gently slurred, the rare sharper ones, as in bars 52–55, have an almost surprising effect in this context. Only with complete inner and outer repose (one thinks of Goethe's letter Zelter[1]) can the player and listener take in the beauty of this prelude, which is no longer a prelude. Half note equals 60 to 63.

The Fugue à 3

Concerning the subject of this fugue Kirnberger remarked that one should play it 'in a fleeting movement, lightly, without the

[1] Quoted in the fly leaf. – Tr.

least pressure.' This is the only instance in which we learn something about the performance of *The Well-Tempered Clavier* from the circle of Bach's students (obviously Kirnberger was thinking of the clavichord). To Riemann, the subject 'leaps up', while David sees in it a body 'which presses forward with heavy links of armor... burrowing violently.' (If further proof were required that the preludes and fugues permit the most varied interpretations, here it is.)

Its delicate charm, which links it with its prelude, is expressed through the choice of the meter as well: in the prelude 3/2, here 6/16. Perhaps it is not without significance that the subject does not begin on the upbeat (like that of the F Sharp Major Fugue in Book II) but with a rest on the beat; this creates problems of balance. With three graceful turns that might almost be called elegant, the subject rises to the octave. On its way back it makes use of a figure much utilized in the Baroque. We find it already in an Organ Toccata in A Major ascribed to Purcell, and Bach himself used it in the Prelude to the First English Suite (BWV 806):

This figure seems to mean more to the composer than the entire subject, for he carries on an amusing play with it. First we note how he takes time before the third voice enters as the tenor, then again as the bass (bar 21) before concluding the first part in bar 29. From this point, the motive described above holds the field alone for 24 bars before the subject at last enters again in the tenor in bar 52. The bass follows in bar 66; the soprano, however, enters only after an exciting preparation through the organpoint on C (bar 85) – its first entry since bar 1 (!). But how it enters: in the minor, accompanied by full harmonies (something unheard of in a three-voiced fugue) and with a powerful eruption to the major, which has the effect of a triumph. The bass expands the first and the second half of the subject over a doubled range (bar 89 ff.) and, accompanied by a joyful dance in the upper voices, leads the fugue to its goal. This cadence reminds one so strongly of the '*largo, ma non tanto*' from the Double Concerto for Two Violins (BWV 1043)

that it seems to be a conscious or unconscious reminiscence of Bach's. Looking back from the end, one may perhaps not regard the beginning of the fugue as so light and free from care as Kirnberger did. The eighth notes in the subject have staccato indications in both Altnikol and Kirnberger. Dotted eighth note equals 96.

BOOK II: NO. 12 IN F MINOR, BWV 881

The Prelude

At the close of the first half of Book II of *The Well-Tempered Clavier* Bach has not, as in Book I, put a specially significant fugue, but the simplest, technically the easiest prelude and the most homophonic fugue – in other words: he has given no particular emphasis to this caesura. One generally sees in this prelude one of Bach's contributions to the *empfindsam* style. When it was written (probably about 1740) Wilhelm Friedemann and Carl Philipp Emanuel had not only already written their first sonatas, but had already published them (while *The Well-Tempered Clavier* had to remain in manuscript). If the father here utilized this style, his inner attitude was quite different. The sighing motives of the prelude are found in excess with the sons, but the clear architecture of this prelude shows the style of the father. After the D Major Prelude this is the second which shows the already developed sonata form: an exposition of $8+12+8=28$ bars; a development-like middle section of $12+12+4=28$ bars; and an abbreviated recapitulation of 14 $(4+2+4+4)$ bars, so that the three parts are related to one another as $2:2:1$. Like the subject of the D Major Prelude, this subject is divided into antecedent (bars 1–4) and consequent (bars 5–8). Did Bach here think of a change of manuals? If the subject reminds one of the style of Bach's sons, the combination of the two motives in the last eight bars of the first part is so ingenious that none of the sons could have written it: the suspension motive lies tied over in the middle voice, the sixteenth notes of bars 5–8 are expanded and carried on in sequences to create the soprano. The two motives are combined with like skill in the development: the chief motive begins, is structured into the answer (bars 33–36) as the middle voice, then continued in freer manner (bars 36 to the middle of 48):

The next eight bars correspond to the last eight of the exposition, the disconnected eighth notes of the upper voice (bars 52–54) showing that this continuation is to be thought of as *diminuendo*. The last bars raise themselves to a painful cry (compare the second movement of the Capriccio on the Journey of a Beloved Brother, BWV 992),

whereupon the prelude sinks to a quiet close.

Since the autograph is lost, we have to depend on the manuscripts of Altnikol and Kirnberger. In bar 32, the former has g′ in the alto, Kirnberger g flat′[1]; in bars 49–50 Altnikol has:

with Kirnberger:

In both cases Kirnberger's reading is probably a later improvement.

Performance: in this prelude the performer must guard especially against a weakly sentimental performance. The expression is objectivized through the form; only the close of

[1] Keller has a double prime here. – Tr.

the development and of the recapitulation call for a freer performance. Quarter note equals 56.

The Fugue à 3

This prelude and fugue are among the most easily understood of Book II of *The Well-Tempered Clavier*. They are closely related: the metrically accented notes f'–e'–b flat'–a flat' of the fugue subject are contained in the first two bars of the prelude; the sequences of bars 9–11 relate closely to those of the prelude (bars 20–24). But how does the fugue maintain the expression of the prelude? Riemann praises its 'enchanting grace and heart-winning loveliness,' David recognizes its ambivalence when speaking of the 'dark merrymaking' of the subject, while other editors have described the fugue as tender, even melancholy. Tovey judged that the fugue demonstrates 'that life without stretti, inversions, and so on can also be beautiful.' What is the truth? In any case the mordent which is in several manuscripts shows that Bach's students conceived the subject with a certain sharpness.

Bach managed the fugue form here as freely as in the following F Sharp Major Fugue. After the exposition (bars 1–17) there are only three more incomplete expositions each of two voices: of soprano and alto in the major (bars 25 and 29, each with an upbeat), of bass and alto (bars 41 and 51) and of soprano and alto (bars 72 and 75). This is however only a matter of academic interest; the musical interest is in the episodes, which give this fugue something of the form of an old classical rondo, and whose sequences are known to us from the prelude:

If this fugue sometimes makes a homophonic impression, it is mainly because of its regular structure. Its subject is 4 bars long like those of the C Minor Fugue in Book I, the B Flat

Major Fugue in Book I and the F Major Fugue in Book II. Of the four episodes (bars 17–24, 33–40, 66–71, and 78–85) three [the first, second and fourth] are regularly of eight bars, while the third, six bars long, is introduced through a passionate, development-like itensification which shows that this fugue is indeed not so innocuous as one might think. In this work, too, Altnikol and Kirnberger have divergent readings in several places, of which Kirnberger's for the most part are to be given preference.

Performance: with caprice and a certain humor which softens, in the episodes, to ease. Quarter note equals 76.

BOOK II: NO. 13 IN F SHARP MAJOR, BWV 882

The Prelude

Bach opens the second half of Book II of *The Well-Tempered Clavier* with a festive prelude. It is in the manner of a French overture and stands in the most extreme contrast to the F sharp Major Prelude in Book I, although it is similar in being only two-voiced. But this is two-voicedness of another sort: it seems to consist merely of the outer voices of a complete orchestral movement, which one may imagine realized in the manner in which Bach executed the last three bars. It has the form of a Baroque concerto movement, and its formal outline is very close to that of the Organ Prelude in C Minor (BWV 546). Its structure is as follows: main section (tonic) bars 1–4, subsidiary section (tonic to dominant) bars 4–17, main section (dominant to subdominant) bars 17–23; subsidiary section bars 23–42 (subdominant to the relative minor), main section (relative minor) bars 42–45, subsidiary section (relative minor to the tonic) bars 45–57, main section (recapitulation) bars 57–60, subsidiary section bars 60–68, coda bars 68–75. The principal subject thus not only holds the main sections together, but remains effective in the subsidiary sections. In this 'concerto in the French style' the main sections and subsidiary sections are not so clearly separated as they are in the Italian Concerto. That the dotted rhythm, with its three following thirty-second notes, must here be performed as in No. 5 of Book I is demonstrated by the vertical alignment of the note heads in Kirnberger's manuscript. The suspension in bar 1, which robs the subject of something of its strength and precision, is found only in copies, not in the autograph. The trills on the leading tone in bars 29–32 and 67 seem already to prepare the trill in the fugue subject.

The performance (best on the harpsichord) requires a certain *grandezza,* but also verve and fire. Quarter note equals 76 to 84.

The Fugue à 3

The bold trill beginning on the leading tone is practically unheard of in a fugue subject; I have not succeeded in finding another example of it among seventeenth and eighteenth-century fugue subjects. The modulation to the subdominant is also uncommon (compare however No. 24 in Book I). When we play on, we believe, in the episodes of bars 23–32 and 56–64, that we have before us a *gavotte* rather than a fugue (one might think perhaps of the one in the Sixth French Suite, BWV 817). This, in short, is a fugue which one cannot measure with preconceived notions (August Halm who does, finds the subject 'paltry,' and the fugue 'uninspired routine'). Busoni was the first to recognize its importance. The subject (a) and the first and second countersubjects (b and c) are in triple counterpoint:

One notes, at the same time, how the subject contains three transpositions of the nuclear upbeat figure (d♯'–e♯'–f♯', c♯'–d♯'–e, b–c♯'–d♯'), that the first countersubject is derived from the close of the subject that the second extends the motive c♯'–d♯'–e' and then associates itself as accompaniment to the subject in such fashion that it seems completely adequate. The gavotte-like episodes also take their leap of a sixth and their suspension motive from the subject itself. How different is the effect here from that in the F Minor Prelude. How modern this fugue is, is shown in its structure: there are 84 bars, namely, 12+12 (exposition and an additional soprano entry in bar 20)+8 (*quasi-gavotte*)+12 (second exposition: bass, alto, soprano)+8 (episode)+4 (subject in the alto) +8 (*quasi-gavotte*)+20 (third exposition: bass bar 64, alto bar 70, soprano bar 76). In addition to the dance-like episode there is a second episode of significance,

whose upper voice takes over the eighth notes of the subject, while its middle voice derives from augmentation of bars 1–2 of the subject. Thus we are charmed not only by the high spirits and the grace with which this fugue continues the mood of its prelude, but equally by its structure, and the playful lightness with which its three voices are closely woven. It is significant that Bach has written out the trill in two places (bars 20 and 70):

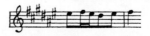

This example demonstrates, first, that generally trills which enter freely begin with the chief note; second, that, the very simple nature of the realization permits us to deduce a lively tempo. The tempo of this fugue may double that of the prelude (thus, half note equals 76 to 84). The gavotte episodes are

commonly played two bars *forte*, two bars *piano*: this while not
specifically marked is entirely in the style of Bach's time.

The Prelude

This prelude must rank among the most important in *The Well-
Tempered Clavier*. It is a great *arioso* whose widespread, noble
melody would unfold its complete beauty only if transcribed
for solo violin accompanied by viola and cello. Mozart, who
did transcribe various movements from *The Well-Tempered
Clavier* for strings (KV 404a and 405), unfortunately overlooked
this beautiful work. It is noticeable that in Book II of *The Well-
Tempered Clavier* (though not yet in Book I) many types of prelude appear in pairs. Thus the preludes in C Sharp Minor
and F Sharp Minor, D Sharp Minor and E Minor, D Major
and B Flat Major, F Sharp Major and A Flat Major are
closely connected. In contrast to the refined sensitivity of the
C Sharp Minor Prelude, that in F Sharp Minor has a quieter,
more concise effect – reminiscent perhaps of a painter of the
Umbrian school, such as Perugino – a comparison expressing
purely the feelings of the author; words indeed cannot convey such shadings. This prelude divides itself into four sections:
the first embraces bars 1–12 (with a phrase-elision in bar 7),
it leads from F sharp minor to C sharp minor. The second
section (bars 12–21) modulates from C sharp minor to A major;
the third (bars 21–29) brings the movement gently to a halt
on a fermata; whereupon the fourth and last section closes the
piece as a recapitulation of the first. Within these four sections
the melody is so firmly conceived as a unit through constant

linking of motives and phrases that one can again echo Wagner:
'the endless melody is here already pre-formed.' The motives
of the first bar – the falling fourth, the undulating movements
of the triplets, the syncopated rhythm – continue their activity
and create that breadth of line in which no Italian has equalled
Bach; it is a technique familiar to every pianist from the
middle movement of the Italian Concerto (BWV 971). Busoni
speaks here of 'a poetry of counterpoint reminiscent of César
Franck.' This prelude is naturally much more than only a
prelude to the fugue; it is also related to it thematically: both
begin with the broken chord of F sharp minor, and the undulating movement of the triplets in the prelude is also found
again, syncopated, in the fugue subject.

Performance: with noble *cantabile* style in all three voices.
Quarter note equals 52.

The Fugue à 3

This fugue is unique in Books I and II of *The Well-Tempered
Clavier*. It is a triple fugue which combines its three subjects
with surpassing mastery in a setting that is only three-voiced;
in so doing it reminds us of The Art of Fugue (BWV 1080),
perhaps of the *Contrapunctus VIII*, which also develops three
subjects in only three voices. Before these two fugues, Bach
had written only one other fugue with three subjects: the five-
voiced Organ Fugue in E Flat Major (BWV 689) which marks
the close of the chorale preludes in the third part of the
Clavierübung. The structure of the organ fugue is A, B, B+A, C,
C+A. In this clavier fugue the structure is: A, B, B+A;
C, C+A+B. In bars 1–20, A alone is developed; in bars
20–28 B alone; in bars 28–36 B+A; in bars 36–51 C alone; in
bar 52 (with upbeat) A is added to C; in bars 55–57 A, B
and C are combined for the first time (A with a variant of its
three upbeat eighth notes), all three are combined for the
second time in bars 60–62. The three themes together are
clearest in the third combination (bar 67 with the upbeat):

Bach may have had this particular combination in mind when he designed the three subjects in relation to each other.

Now however to the subjects themselves. The first is admirably poised. The line c sharp'–f sharp–d' is juxtaposed with the altered form f sharp'–b–a in bars 2–3; the two syncopated motives which surround the steps d' to c sharp and b to a are framed on the one hand by the opening three upbeat eighth notes and on the other, by the final trill. With partial motives from the subject, a capricious play is carried on in the episodes; the fall of the fifth f sharp–b is imitated between two voices (bar 7), the three upbeat eighth notes in their original form as well as in inversion are used for enveloping the subject in the bass, and they simulate entries through which the listener is led astray. With Schwencke the second subject has a *pralltrill* over the dotted eighth note which gives it a clearer profile and makes it easier for us to follow. Subject A is twice added to subject B: in bar 29 with an upbeat in the alto, and in bar 34 in the bass. Subject C possesses little individual personality; it describes (similar to the second subject in the C Sharp Minor Fugue in Book I) a slowly descending movement. Against it, too, parts of A enter incessantly until the whole of this subject appears complete in the alto beginning in bar 52 (with an upbeat). In the sixteenth notes of bars 54–55 the eighth note upbeat of the fugue subject is hidden:

similarly in the bass in bar 60.

This fugue affords a high intellectual pleasure to him who penetrates its compositional technique. However, it gives more. The fugue's chief subject is of ambivalent character, at once thoughtful and capricious; the second subject is terse, energetic; the third, gently flowing. All three join together to a higher unity in a fashion which is possible in no art other than music. Of this fugue Busoni said: 'The content is, with all wisdom, full of youth; the intellectual stands side by side with the emotional.' To combine all of this into a unity of satisfying sound is no easy job for the performer. Quarter note equals 84.

BOOK II: NO. 15 IN G MAJOR, BWV 884

The Prelude

Bach wrote no fewer than three preludes to the most unpretentious fugue of *The Well-Tempered Clavier*. The first prelude and the fugue in its first form, entitled *Fughetta*, were probably written as early as during Bach's first Cöthen years. This prelude (BWV 902a) numbered 33 (16+17) bars.

It is rich in sequences which are paralleled in the ensuing *fughetta*. Later, probably in Leipzig, Bach discarded this prelude and prefaced the *fughetta* with a new, large, two-part prelude (BWV 902):

With its 28+28 measures and a recapitulation in the second part, this work has the same form as the large two-part preludes in Book II of *The Well-Tempered Clavier* and thus would be counted among the most significant of its kind had it not in turn been discarded by Bach, probably because its size and significance would have smothered the little fugue. When Bach decided to put the *fughetta* into *The Well-Tempered Clavier*, he went back to the first prelude, which he now entirely reworked. Both parts were provided with repetitions and the second part was doubled in size to 32 (= 12+8+12) bars. Now it has become a masterpiece which combines youth and maturity. It has so youthfully fresh an effect that it could form the prelude of the Fifth French Suite (BWV 816) (compare No. 9 in Book I) and from the point of view of compositional technique, it is stunningly worked. 'Everything beautiful treads on light feet.' Since grace and haste are not compatible, as von Bülow once remarked, one must not play it *allegro vivace*, as many editions prescribe (quarter note equals 132); the turns in bars 13, 27 and 45 should hold us back from that. Light, almost unnoticeable caesuras are needed after the third eighth note in bars 2, 3, 5, 6 and – in the bass – bars 9–11. Quarter note equals 96.

The Fugue à 3

This fugue, in the elaboration of its subject the simplest, in its polyphony the most free of *The Well-Tempered Clavier*, has one of the longest subjects and, as regards compass – it spans an eleventh – the widest range. Thus the length of this fugue is in amusing disproportion to the length of the subject. Moreover the subject itself, a garland woven from broken triads and seventh chords, permits no serious working out.

After the exposition, the complete subject enters only three more times: bar 33 (second note) in the bass, bar 40 in the soprano (an incomplete re-exposition in minor) and at the close (bar 65) in the alto. The figuration of the first version was enriched, and the second part was extended through the insertion of bars 53–64. The sequences land on an organpoint on D (bars 56–62), which is enlivened through trills; thereupon the soprano rises in an elegant run over three octaves, the alto adds the subject, and then the soprano takes the lead again and closes the delicate play with a roguish bow.

In its reworking the fugue was improved in almost every bar, refined in expression, and made worthy of its prelude.

Performance: delicately moving, neither hurried nor hasty. The suspension on the final note is an eighth note, by analogy with bars 25, 27, etc. Dotted quarter note equals 48.

BOOK II: NO. 16 IN G MINOR, BWV 885

The Prelude

This prelude, one of the most characteristically Baroque, is in G minor, the typical Baroque key; it resembles organ music in style, and employs throughout the dotted rhythm so beloved of Handel (cf. the preludes to his Suites in F Minor and F Sharp Minor). It is the only piece in Book II of *The Well-Tempered Clavier* that has a tempo indication, *largo*, which (as in the case of the B Minor Fugue in Book I) signifies less a tempo than the *grandezza* of Baroque pathos. This would make a Bach *Organo pleno* most suitable for this prelude. Nevertheless, there is no cold pomp, but an animated *cantabile* quality in its polyphony. For this reason the dotted rhythm is not to be played in the jagged fashion of a French Overture. One may argue whether to double-dot the eighth notes in the usual Baroque style (e.g. in the tenor in bars 3 and 4, and by analogy in later places) or whether (as Busoni suggests) the sixteenth notes and the thirty-second notes should be sharply differentiated, which would momentarily relax the rhythmic monotony.

If one looks at this prelude as a consistent four-voiced structure, the alto enters first in the middle of bar 3; but as in the
Prelude in C Major in Book II, Bach is here thinking in terms
of a keyboard instrument, not from the point of view of voice-
leading. In the very first bar of the Prelude the outline of the
opening measure of the fugue subject is already recognizable,
and the a–d'–b flat in bars 2–3[1] of the fugue are a transformation of the soprano in bar 2 of the prelude. The inner connection
is stronger and needs no further evidence.

Performance: with a fullness of sound and, notwithstanding
pathos, with singable expression. Eighth note equals 76 to 84.
(According to Riemann half note equals 40!)

The Fugue à 4

The series of six three-voiced fugues (Nos. 10 through 15) is
now followed by a four-voiced one, and one of great style. The
prelude has served as an introduction,[2] whose concealed
strengths are released and expanded in the fugue. The fugue
subject is a declamation with raised voice, like a hurled protest.
The six repeated eighth notes sound as if someone were beating
with his fist on a table (the square brackets in the opening
example clarify that the subject does not consist of isolated
outcries but represents a coherent speech; the first note is a
beginning *ex abrupto*). In opposition to the subject, the countersubject enters, first rising passionately then ponderously rolling
down.

Both subjects require a big fugue in which to measure their
strengths against each other. There are no stretti, as they would
weaken the forcefulness of the subject; and the episodes are
restricted to minimum essentials. Bach here makes use of another

---

[1] Keller: 2. – Tr.
[2] Keller uses here the German word *Vorspiel*, rather than 'prelude.'

artistic device which we meet again in Book II of *The Well-Tempered Clavier* only in the B Flat Minor Fugue: viz. the doubling of the subject and countersubject in thirds and sixths.

The exposition (which modulates to D minor) extends to bar 25,[1] since the additional entry in the tenor (bar 20) must be regarded as part of it. The second exposition (bars 28–45) is distinguished from the first and the third through its mere three-voiced texture; it therefore contains only three entries of the subject (alto bar 28, soprano bar 32, bass bar 36); the tenor is left out so that, accompanied by the alto in thirds in bar 45, it can introduce the third exposition. This doubling in thirds, prepared in bars 37 and 38, doubles the rhetorical strength of the subject; soprano and alto (bar 51) follow in sixths, tenor and bass in bar 59 in thirds. Here the polyphony simplifies to give to the countersubject the opportunity to fortify itself with thirds so that both subjects collide in full force. After this concentration, there is a break (bar 67) after which subject and countersubject are led against each other in tenths; and with the hemiola of bars 73–74 the end seems to have been reached. But it is only after a second extension of the close (bars 75–79) that we become convinced that this increasingly exultant fugue must sometime have an end. Space forbids that we should trace all the elaborate developments to which the countersubject is subjected.

No stringed keyboard instrument can adequately do justice to the expression of this fugue with its cumulative rhetoric. Probably this is the reason why it is so rarely played. It is difficult to maintain the tension from beginning to end, and the player is in danger of wearing himself out too soon. Quarter note equals 72.

BOOK II: NO. 17 IN A FLAT MAJOR, BWV 886

The history of this prelude and fugue, as we can reconstruct it, is interesting and complicated. When he was at Cöthen, Bach had written a prelude with a *fughetta* in F major (BWV 901). Needing a piece in A flat major for Book II of *The Well-Tempered Clavier*, he retrieved this *fughetta*, transposed it into

[1] Keller: 26. – Tr.

A flat major by the simple expedient of substituting the treble clef for the original soprano clef in the upper staff. This involved changing only the key signature, as the notes remained the same. Hence this is the only work in the whole of the 48 notated in the treble clef (for the sake of uniformity, subsequent editions transposed it back into the soprano clef). Bach doubled the length of the fugue and wrote a large, new prelude for it. Their close relationship is clear from the similar end Bach gives to both, better observed from a look at the fugue.

The Prelude

This prelude exemplifies Bach's mature style. The form of the Baroque concerto movement is here intellectualized to the last detail. The fluency of the transitions and the dovetailing of the various sections of the work make one feel that here Bach transcends the Baroque concerto form in much the same way as Beethoven does the sonata form in his Sonatas Opus 101 to 111. The prelude has a uniquely powerful momentum, contained at the close and arrested by a hemiola. The contours of the structure are: chief section (tonic) bars 1–6, subsidiary section (tonic to dominant) bars 7–16, chief section (dominant) bars 17–22, subsidiary section (dominant to relative minor) bars 23–33, chief section (relative minor) bars 34–39, subsidiary section (relative minor to subdominant) bars 40–49, chief section (subdominant) bars 50–63, coda bars 64–77. The kinship of this prelude in form and expression with the F Sharp Major Prelude is obvious, though it surpasses that prelude in its unity and workmanship. Here Bach uses the more exact notation ♪♫♫ in place of the ♪.♫♫ which he had used in the D Major Fugue in Book I and the F Sharp Major Prelude in Book II. The two suspensions in the third-from-last bar are not in the autograph but are taken from Altnikol, whose copy incorporates various improvements: ought one however to regard the addition of these suspensions in this magnificent majestic piece as an improvement?

Performance: with grandeur and dignity, but not stiff and ponderous, in the Baroque *tempo ordinario*. Quarter note equals 63 to 66.

The Fugue à 4

As explained, this fugue consists of two halves of which the second was composed about twenty years after the first. But the latter half is so closely bound to the first that no one would notice the joints which lie between bars 23 and 24. The first part, originally in F major, is indeed so richly provided with thematic material that the expressive power of the two subjects could not be fully realized in a mere 23 bars; it is also unsatisfactory that only in the two final bars does it really become four-voiced. In its elaboration for *The Well-Tempered Clavier* the opening half seems to be no more than a widely extended exposition. The subject combines grace, equipoise and solemnity. Although it has an upbeat, fourths play a decisive role in its structure (see the square brackets in the musical example); the middle axis is the octave e flat″–e flat′; the eighth notes c″–b flat′–e flat″–c″ (contained within the sixteenth notes) at the close balance the four eighth notes at the beginning. To this quiet and widely ranging subject is added an obbligato counterpoint with a chromatic *ductus*, which takes on the importance of a second subject, so that one can view this fugue as a double fugue with two subjects connected from the beginning even if in two places (bars 16–17 and 32–33) the first subject enters without the second.

This type of double fugue is found only in the youthful works of Bach (in the toccatas and in the Cantata BWV 131); a chromatic second subject already occurs in the Double Fugue in A Minor (BWV 904). To the two characteristic subjects is added, mediating and reconciling, a counterpoint in gentle sixteenth-note movement which also provides the few episodes which occur. In the first part a second exposition of all four voices follows the first (bass bar 13, alto bar 16, tenor bar 18,

soprano bar 22). By this time one should be intrigued to see
how Bach will develop his material. The way in which he
casually allows the tenor voice to disappear in bar 24 until its
reappearance with the subject in minor in bar 32 is still characteristic of the style of the opening section of the fugue. Otherwise, in the second half, the fugue is filled with ever-growing
seriousness, turning toward the minor and the darker keys: in
the third exposition beginning with the alto entry in F minor
(bar 24) we continue with the tenor in E flat minor (bar 32),
soprano in B flat minor (bar 35[1]), and bass in D flat major
(bar 37). A fourth exposition in which only tenor (bar 41) and
bass (bar 42) take part, leads in a dramatic intensification (in
whose jagged basses we are reminded of the organ pedal) to a
breaking off on the first inversion of the dominant seventh
chord. Then the fugue closes, majestic and solemn, in a coda
in which the double subject enters once more in a five-voiced
texture, but so hidden in the middle voices that neither eye nor
ear can recognize its entry easily:

Performance: strictly legato, without caesuras in the subject;
in the second half, intensifying; in the tempo of the prelude.
Quarter note equals 60 to 63.

BOOK II: NO. 18 IN G SHARP MINOR, BWV 887

Probably these two pieces also were sketched in G minor and
only subsequently transposed into the higher key, which now
lends them a special charm.

The Prelude

From its two-part organization (24 + 26 bars) one might think
this prelude an *allemande*, but not from its character. It is nearer

[1] Keller: 25. – Tr.

to the *galant* style than to a conventional old suite movement; and like many preludes in Book II, it shows traits of the early Classic sonata form. The first part could be a sonata exposition in which the reappearance of the chief subject replaces the usual second subject, but transposed to the dominant (a procedure which we still find with Haydn). In the second part, bars 25–40 can be regarded as the development section; the abbreviated recapitulation begins in the bass in bar 40, and in the soprano in bar 41. It occupies only ten instead of twelve bars because there is no repetition of the opening two bars. For this repeat, Bach himself prescribes *piano* in bar 3, followed by *forte* in bar 5. This makes it reasonable to suppose that Bach here had a harpsichord with two manuals in mind, and it would be worthwhile making such a distribution throughout the entire prelude (for it is an unlikely assumption that Bach wished to confine this treatment to these two measures). The regular structure of the work as a whole is interspersed with charming little irregularities. The 24 bars of the first part divide themselves into 15 $(4+3+3+5)+9$ $(2+3+4)$ bars, the second part into 16 $(7+4+5)+10$ $(2+4+4)$ bars. How many clever linkages, extensions, elisions of phrases and motives are hidden behind these bare numbers! In bar 31 the appoggiaturas, missing in all manuscripts, should be provided. The fugue shares and intensifies the *galant* style of the prelude; both subjects hover round the tonic and the dominant; the beginning notes of the prelude are also those of the fugue subject.

Performance: animated, but not too lively, with a certain elegance. Quarter note equals 84.

The Fugue à 3

This fugue should be judged by criteria different from those we apply to most of Bach's other fugues. Its subject 'glides with lizard-like nimbleness in triplet eighth notes' (Riemann), its rocking gently rising and falling movement dominates the entire fugue, which consequently is almost devoid of rhythmic contrast. The subject, which merely transposes the first two bars one whole tone upward, has the effect not of a complete idea but more of an antecedent to which the following four bars (of counterpoint) form the consequent. The contrast of the purely diatonic subject with the entirely chromatic countersubject permeates the entire fugue. It is a double fugue ('two-theme fugue'), whose second subject, entering in bar 61, with its chromatic *ductus*, is so closely akin to the countersubject that one scarcely realizes anything new has occurred; indeed one would hardly notice the second subject as such at all were it not given a little more profile through its final trill.

With any other fugue, one would count this a weakness; here however it is obvious that Bach did not intend creating thematic contrast, but only to reinforce the chromatic contrast to the first subject. As a result the combination of the two themes is not felt as an eagerly expected and then welcome event; with the entry of the two subjects together (from bar 97) the fugue in no way alters the gently flowing character which it maintains to the end. It closes without any outer or inner intensification, as it began. Also striking is the regularity of its metric structure, which is not to be explained simply by the four bars of its subject. The complete fugue numbers 144 bars (the closing bar counted doubled); exactly at the beginning of the final third of the fugue (bar 97) the two subjects combine; after the first 60 bars, the second subject enters, so that the three parts of the fugue are related exactly as 5:3:4.

Its structure can be schematized as follows:

> Exposition of the first subject, bars 1–32 (with an additional alto entry in bar 19), modulation to D sharp minor.
> Second exposition: entries separated through larger episodes: bars 33–60 (bass bar 33, soprano bar 45, bass in a low position bar 55).
> Second fugue subject: bars 61–96 (soprano bar 61, alto bar 66, bass 71, higher soprano bar 79).[1]

---

[1] Keller: 73 – Tr.

Combination of both the subjects (bars 97–144): bass and alto bar 97, soprano and alto bar 103, alto and soprano bar 111, alto and bass bar 125, soprano and alto bar 135.

Since each of the two subjects occupies only four bars, ample space remains for episodes in which segments of motives of both subjects are combined.

Performance: this fugue is effective only with a nimble, fluent tempo; everything is legato, the dynamics do not exceed *mf*. Dotted quarter note equals 96 or more.

BOOK II: NO. 19 IN A MAJOR, BWV 888

The Prelude

Over this prelude shines the spring-like brilliance of the key of A major. Its meter (12/8) shows it to be a *pastorale*; in the nature of its working-out, it is a three-part invention. It is closely related to the prelude of the First English Suite (BWV 806). Both are in the same key and meter, of equal length, and develop their respective subjects in similar fashion. The subject of the Suite (compare page 164) descends a sixth, that of the prelude ascends a sixth.

The motive which is the basis of this prelude is handled in much the same way as that of the three-part sinfonia in E Major (BWV 792). The soprano intones it, the alto takes it up, in bar 3 the bass follows; then intertwining, the two upper voices elaborate it further. In bar 6, the third voice continues the bass in the tenor range. In bars 9–10 the bass, soprano, alto and bass again[1] follow one another with the inversion of the subject; in bars 11–15 the alto, bass and soprano answer with the subject in its original form and close the first part in F sharp minor (bar 16). The second part is similarly constructed; the sections flow so gently into each other that the listener believes he hears three blessed voices in unity.

[1] Keller omits mention of the additional statement in the bass. The phrase 'and bass again' has been added by the translator.

Performance: with quiet delicacy. Dotted quarter note equals 72.

The Fugue à 3

This fugue is one of the simplest and least pretentious of *The Well-Tempered Clavier*. The subject, in three stairsteps, with a pause on each, ascends to the fifth and sinks back to the third. In its constantly intertwining motives, the subject recalls the prelude; it can easily be discovered in the leading of the soprano in the first three bars of the prelude. The fugue substitutes a quiet walk for the dance step of the prelude. The countersubject slips itself in dotted rhythm between the syncopations of the subject; but it is not in itself of great significance, and for that reason it is the ending of the subject (the last eight notes) that forms the basis of the episodes. The structure, too, of this fugue scarcely calls for comment. To the exposition (bars 1–6) is added immediately a second exposition in the order bass (bar 7), soprano (bar 9) and alto (bar 12), the last two in the minor. The second part of the fugue (from bar 16) offers only one more widely separated exposition of bass (bar 16), soprano (bar 20) and alto (bar 23); and in the coda, introduced with animation, a final entry of the soprano. In bar 16 the contrabass A is required. This is the first time in Books I and II of *The Well-Tempered Clavier* that the low C has been exceeded (this happens again at the close of the B Major Prelude and the B Minor Fugue). One remarkable feature distinguishes this fugue from all the others of Bach (not only within *The Well-Tempered Clavier*): viz. that the subject, from its entry in bar 9 on, enters with the upbeat lengthened by a note. The tempo of the fugue may be the same as that of the prelude. Quarter note equals 72.

BOOK II: NO. 20 IN A MINOR, BWV 889

The Prelude

This astonishing prelude was constructed by Bach the mathematician. It is a two-part invention of a strictness that exceeds that of all other two-part instrumental movements of Bach. One can study it as a blueprint design: two exactly similar halves of 16 bars each; in the first section of the second half (bars 17–24) the two subjects, firmly and indissolubly bound together, are inverted; in the second section (bars 25–32) they are combined in normal and inverted movement. The eighth notes falling chromatically from a to e can be regarded as the main theme of the movement, a series of notes with which both Bach and his contemporaries expressed a painful *Affekt*, for example in the Lament from the Capriccio on the Journey of His Beloved Brother (BWV 992), and in the ostinato bass of the Cantata BWV 12 '*Weinen, Klagen*' and the *Crucifixus* of the B Minor Mass (BWV 232). Here, in *The Well-Tempered Clavier*, in the rarefied atmosphere of reflection, the chromaticism has lost its affective significance. Against this motion in the bass, the upper part seems to speak with two voices. We hear chromatically falling sixth chords (the chromatic neighboring notes of this expressive melody make it possible for the texture to be inverted without producing a series of 6/4 chords).

The combination of the two subjects occupies exactly half the measures of the first section (bars 1–2, 4–5, 8–9, 11 and 13); the remaining 8 bars (3, 6, 7, 10, 12 and 14–16) are devoted to a half-bar motive whose upper voice is built from a variation of the falling soprano, while the diatonically rising eighth notes invert the bass of bar 1.

In the second section, the chief subject appears in inversion in both voices in bars 17–18[1] and 21–22;[2] in bars 25–26 its normal form is followed by the inverted one, in bars 30–31 this process is reversed – symmetries which need to be observed visually. The half-bar motive is also inverted in the second section in both voices (bars 19–20 and 23–24); in bar 26 it appears in its normal form and is extended to three bars; the last bar 32 is free.

This prelude is intellectual music of the highest order. Kirnberger used it as an example in his pamphlet '*Die wahren Grundsätze zum Gebrauch der Harmonie*' (The Real Basis for the Use of Harmony) which appeared in 1773; it was the first prelude of *The Well-Tempered Clavier* to appear in print. Whether Kirnberger succeeded in solving that riddle of this sphinx is open to doubt. The prelude stands like a guard before the fugue, holding back forces which the latter will release.

Performance: in strict, reflective *legato*, yet with caesurae after the first, or first and fifth eighth notes of the subject. Not *pp* (Czerny) but in an objective manner with little change in tone quality. Eighth note equals 63 to 66 (like the quarter note of the fugue).

The Fugue à 3

This fugue is an extraordinary outburst of temper: it 'represents an individual man and he rages!' (David). The quarter notes fall like hammer blows, split into eighth notes like tumbling rocks; the torn thirty-second notes and the rolling trill of the countersubject complete the picture of a storm – a psychic one, for Bach wrote no pastoral symphonies. This fugue does not bother with academic rules. Its subject, which alone in the second volume of *The Well-Tempered Clavier* modulates to the dominant, is never heard in its original form after its first appearance. It reappears either with an altered close (bars

[1] Keller: 16–17. – Tr.
[2] Keller: 20–21. – Tr.

14–15 in the soprano, bars 26–27 in the bass) or shortened
to four eighth notes in the consequent (according to Czaczkes
this is the true form of the subject, though only when the other
voices continue the consequent through sequences as in bars
11–13, 19–20 and 23–24). The outline of this subject was
common property in this period. It is found in Handel's
Messiah

And with His stripes we are heal - ed.

and in the Finale of the F Minor Quartet Opus 20 by Haydn
(Hoboken III: 35); nowhere however does it appear with such
elemental power as in *The Well-Tempered Clavier*. The
quarter notes must be heavily set apart, the eighth notes more
sharply marked. The autograph carries no staccato signs over
the eighth notes. These occur only in the manuscripts of
Kirnberger (as wedges) and Schwencke (as dots). The fugue
closes in the major and we have no right, as Tovey would, to
alter the close to the minor.

As regards the text, in Altnikol the bass is transposed up an
octave in bar 15 (perhaps to avoid the clattering sound of the
harpsichord in the lower register?); in bar 6 Altnikol's version

is easier to play than that of the autograph:

This fugue is in extreme contrast with its prelude, although its
subject is foreshadowed in the first bar of the prelude in the
upper voice.

Performance: heavy and powerful, therefore not too fast.
Quarter note equals 63 to 66 (the doubled tempo of the prelude).

BOOK II: NO. 21 IN B FLAT MAJOR, BWV 890

The Prelude

This prelude is a round dance of indescribable grace: how the voices rise and fall, become interwoven, separate themselves again! – and at the same time it is a sonata movement so highly developed as to be very close to a Classic sonata form. The hint of a second subject, which was still missing in the preludes in D Major and F Minor, is here recognizable. The chief subject (4+4 bars) modulates to the dominant. Then, in bars 9–12, the two intermingled voices

could be regarded as a second subject; its continuation (bars 13–16) with the crossing of the two hands is so similar to a passage in the C Minor Fantasy (BWV 906), composed in 1738, that the prelude may well date from the same time. In the continuation, as often with the Viennese classic composers, the first subject is again referred to (bar 21); and the closing group with its turn to the minor (bar 28) ends the exposition, regularly built throughout with thirty-two bars. The development section (as the middle section may here properly be called) is connected to the closing group, stretches on through the passage where the hands cross (which is omitted in the recapitulation) and closes after sixteen bars in G minor. The recapitulation (from bar 49) reduces the first sixteen bars of the exposition to eight, but extends the consequent and brings the movement to a halt on the third inversion of the dominant seventh chord (bar 76). Then, with a 'general upbeat' (bars 76 to 81, where one is reminded of the upbeat occupying several bars in the first movement of the Sonata Op. 31 No. 3 of Beethoven) we arrive at a passage corresponding to the closing group of the exposition. Thus this prelude also grows beyond itself in this second part, giving up its detached attitude.

In this respect too it is nearer to the Viennese classic style than to the older music to which it is still bound through its technique, the true three-voiced texture. Any disproportion between this important, large-scale prelude and the little fugue which follows is only illusory. The prelude, with its regular meter (12/16)[1] may be regarded as the principal dance; the fugue, in its winged 3/4 meter, as the "after-dance" (*Nachtanz*). They are moreover interconnected through their common chief motive, the falling sixth.

Performance: in gentle, flowing movement, without any haste. Dotted eighth note equals 80 to 84.

The Fugue à 3

The subject of this fugue is unique in preclassic literature as it begins on the ninth of the key, even if this ninth is only the neighboring note to the octave. The subject, put together from four single-bar motives (a a b b), delicately descends, in two terraces, from the octave to the tonic, and continues in caressing eighth-note motives. The fugue consists of two parts of unequal length: bars 1–32 and 32–93. Both parts have the same concluding section of four bars and this very fact makes it plain that this fugue is not to be considered purely as a piece of counterpoint. Yet the fugue is that, too. At the beginning of the second part, two new countersubjects (b) and (c) attach themselves to the subject, which until then had shown no special needs.

They enter in the second bar of the subject creating a three-part texture in triple counterpoint: in bar 33 the combination is b–a–c, in bar 41 a–c–b, bar 49 c–b–a, bar 56 c–a–b (here b

and c enter a bar later), in bars 64–80 a–b–c. Yet these contrapuntal permutations are handled in an indolent, almost casual,
manner, in no way disturbing the serene unconcern of the
fugue.

Performance: lightly animated, with grace and some humor.
Quarter note equals 120 (1½ times the tempo of the prelude).

BOOK II: NO. 22 IN B FLAT MINOR, BWV 891

The Prelude

Where contrapuntal art and intellectual discipline are concerned, the prelude and fugue in B Flat Minor must be
regarded as the peak of Book II of *The Well-Tempered Clavier*.
They do not make it easy either for the player or the listener.
The prelude, a three-part invention – the greatest Bach wrote –
rejects any rhythmic and harmonic embellishment; and to
listen attentively to this fugue is no less exciting than it is to
listen to the fugue in Beethoven's *Hammerklavier* Sonata. Anyone who penetrates into it, however, has taken a look into
Bach's workshop, as the player of Beethoven's Sonatas Opus
106–111 can look into the creative process of the Viennese
master. Already the subject is of unusual breadth. In its complete form it first appears in the soprano (bar 8):

Here only one can suspect its full beauty, but in its entirety,
it is only found once more (in the alto, bars 62–70). Busoni
has pointed out that the melodic line of its first section is
similar to that of the B Flat Major Fugue. Despite their
extreme contrast, such a resemblance is not impossible, and
it is conceivable that they were composed one after the other.

The (perhaps unconscious) reminiscence of the B Flat Minor Prelude in Book I is even more striking.

The structure of this invention is as follows: the exposition (bars 1–30) is of extraordinary length. The alto begins, the soprano follows in bar 8, the bass enters with the subject only in bar 25. The second exposition (bars 31–54) is in the major. The soprano enters in bar 31 in D flat major; in bar 42 in A flat major, the subject appears in the bass, who passes it on after only two bars to the alto who continues it; similarly the entry of the alto in bar 48 (in G flat major) is taken up by the soprano after two bars. The third and last exposition (bars 55–83) contains only two more entries of the subject: bar 55 in the soprano in E flat minor and bar 62 in the alto in B flat minor; then it continues in a climax over an organpoint on the dominant (bars 73–76) and closes without broaching the subject once again. The subject is provided with two countersubjects which surround it in eighth-note movement. These eighth notes also create the material of the episodes. In bars 5 and 6, bar 1 of the soprano is inverted in the bass.

On the whole, segments of the subject and countersubject are deployed in every bar.

Performance: slur the eighth notes strictly, separate the quarter notes firmly; a very quiet, but not dragging tempo. Half note equals 56.

The Fugue à 4

There are four fugues in Book II of *The Well-Tempered Clavier* in which in varying degrees contrapuntal devices put in an appearance: two of vocal character in major (D major and

E major), two instrumental in minor (G minor and B flat minor). The power of expression of the B Flat Minor Fugue is so great that no instrument, least of all the harpsichord, can be adequate in regard to sonority; one might wish for chorus and orchestra (a Bach cantata orchestra) for its aural realization. The B Flat Minor Fugue fulfills the promise given by the A Minor Fugue in Book I. Its entire strength comes from the subject, which rises heavy and troubled, from the tonic to the supertonic in two half notes, is persuaded to walk in quarter notes, coaxed into freer movement in eighth notes, and finally reaches its goal: the fifth of the scale (compare the subjects of the F Sharp Minor Fugue in Book I and the D Sharp Minor Fugue in Book II). These three attacks of the subject are not (as with the D Sharp Minor Fugue) tied over, but separated through rests, pauses for breath which the subject needs to summon new strength. The final turn in the fourth bar is a variant of the second bar.

Two countersubjects attend it throughout the fugue; the first

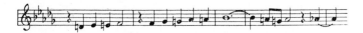

pursues it with chromatic steps; the second

punctuates the eighth notes of the subject with heavy blows, reminding one again of the Cantata BWV 102 (*'Du schlägest sie, aber sie fühlen es nicht'*). The three subjects combine to provide the fugue with an abundance of sorrowful gestures, which are however objectivized and sublimated through the fugal work, as we found in Book I of *The Well-Tempered Clavier* with the fugues in F minor and B minor. Here, however, Bach makes it still more difficult for us because in the working out of the subject he uses exclusively the rarest and most dissonant forms of imitation, namely those at the seventh and ninth. At these intervals the subject loses its harmonic identity without taking on a new one; these imitations must therefore be followed contrapuntally more faithfully than in any other Bach fugue. Even reading this fugue is not easy, because the entries of the subject are hardly visible to the eye, still less perceptible to the ear, for Bach has rejected giving them any sort of prominence. One is therefore obliged to study this fugue in three stages: first the clarification of the text, second, that of the contrapuntal work, third, of its content.

For the first stage, the construction of the fugue is here briefly sketched: exposition (bars 1–26[1]) in the order alto, soprano, bass, tenor. Second exposition with stretto at the minimum distance, i.e. a half note, at the seventh: tenor and alto bar 27.

The soprano and bass follow at the ninth below (as the inversion of the seventh) in bar 33. In the third exposition (bars 42–66) the subject, without being strettoed, is inverted. The tenor enters in bar 42, the alto in bar 46, the soprano in bar 52, the bass in bar 58. The fourth exposition (bars 67[2]–79) combines the features of the second and third: the subject is simultaneously inverted and strettoed at the ninth (as the inversion of the seventh): bar 67 between tenor and soprano (again at the distance of a half note),

bar 73 between alto and bass at the seventh below. The sixth exposition (bars 80–95) brings the one remaining combination: a stretto in which the leading voice is answered by the imitating voice in contrary motion.

In bar 80, soprano and tenor enter in this relationship; in bar 89, bass and alto. In the final exposition, the voices shed all accessories, double their strength in a similar fashion as we saw

[1] Keller: 25. – Tr.
[2] Keller: 49. – Tr.

at the close of the G Minor Fugue, and enter in opposed pairs, soprano and alto together against bass and tenor in contrary motion (bar 96):

With this lapidary coda, Bach concludes the most powerful fugue of *The Well-Tempered Clavier.* Busoni calculated that Bach did not by any means utilize all the possible combinations of the subject. He noted no fewer than seven ways in normal and an equal number in contrary motion in which the imitating voice might enter 1, 2 or 3 half notes after the first voice. But Bach's accomplishment is based on the premise of limiting his imitation to a time distance of a half note and an intervallic distance of the seventh and ninth. Had he not restricted himself to the latter, the parallel movement of the eighth notes (bar 3 of the subject) could not have been maintained.

So far we have spoken only of those sections of the fugue devoted to the subject. For the remaining sections, which are inadequately described as 'episodes', the countersubjects and the closing motive of the subject are mostly brought into play (the latter especially in bars 21–24). The chromatic countersubject also participates in the inversion of the subject, while the struck chords of the second countersubject remain associated with the eighth notes of the subject. If one surveys the entire fugue and compares it with the A Minor Fugue in Book I probably composed more than twenty years earlier, one sees what a distance Bach has travelled in this time. What variety of rhythms compared with the monotony of the A Minor Fugue, what compression of the form! One should play this fugue only for someone who can read along in the score, for the ear alone will not succeed in grasping the details of its construction. August Halm has given a full appreciation of the fugue in his *Zwei Kulturen der Musik* (Two Musical Cultures). Even in the best performance it remains almost as resistant as Beethoven's Fugues in Opus 106 and 133. The tempo ought not be too slow, perhaps half note equals 72.

BOOK II: NO. 23 IN B MAJOR, BWV 892

The Prelude

An entire world separates this prelude from the preceding one. It is so youthful and cavalier-like that one thinks more of the *Kapellmeister* in Cöthen than of the Cantor in Leipzig. It is a *concertante* piece which, while making no pretense at being a worked-out concerto movement like the preludes in F Sharp Major and A Flat Major in Book II, is more than a toccata-like preamble. It has only one relative in *The Well-Tempered Clavier*: the G Sharp Minor Prelude in Book II, from which many features are lifted almost literally. It is divided into four sections: bars 1–12, 12–23, 24 (with upbeat)–36, and (as a shortened recapitulation of the first part) bars 37–46. The predominantly two-voice structure expands to three voices in the imitatively developed bars 12–15 and 24–28; it is reduced to a single voice in their toccata-like continuation. The division of the passage work between the two hands is the signature of the youthful Bach: after 1730 we no longer find this technique, which serves to give the passage work more brilliance and color.

Brandt-Buys, as well as David, has sought to demonstrate a thematic connection with the fugue. I see it in the first passage which storms from the tonic to its octave, a goal which in the fugue is reached with quiet steps; and in the final chord, whose range the fugue subject fills precisely. One can further imagine the third B–d sharp of the fugue subject in the rise of the third b′–c sharp″–d sharp″ of the subject of the prelude; but these relationships are very fleeting. On the other hand, the motive in bar 3 may point to a relationship of the motive

with that of bar 4 of the F Sharp Major Prelude or, still further back, with the accompanying motive in the middle section of the Fifth Brandenburg Concerto, BWV 1050 (first movement). But we forget all these formal considerations if we let ourselves be carried along by the energy and *élan* of this brilliant piece. It is an ideal harpsichord piece, in the rapidly, thrown-away close of which one can almost envisage the player taking his hands from the keyboard, pushing back his chair, and the listeners breaking into applause. Correspondingly the performance must be fiery, richly-colored. Quarter note equals 96 to 100.

The Fugue à 4

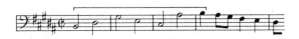

The subject of this fugue lifts itself in quiet, ceremonial steps in intervals of the third and sixth from the tonic to the octave, and in so doing traverses the same distance as the opening of the prelude in one fiery dash. It could be a choral subject in a Mass intoned by the bass; it has a gentle euphony which is shared by the entire fugue. As in the C Sharp Minor Fugue in Book I, the voices enter in the order bass, tenor, alto, soprano; a syncopated countersubject

further strengthens the onward rising movement. After an additional entry of the bass (bar 19) the first part of the fugue closes in bar 27 with an intimate turn to the dominant. Now it takes a surprising turn. A new subject, floating down from above, combines with the first one and accompanies it from here to the end (with the exception of a bass entry in bar 75), giving the impression of a double fugue:

The two subjects are combined not only at the octave, but also at the 12th:

Its two-voiced structure is based exclusively on thirds and sixths, and hence exudes a gentle harmonious quality recalling the double fugue of the Organ Toccata in F Major (BWV 540). The two subjects twice run in this combination through all four voices of the fugue. The second exposition (the first after the initial exposition) combines tenor and soprano in bars 27–28, alto and bass in bars 35–36, soprano and alto in bars 42–43, bass and soprano in bars 48–49, the second subject always entering one bar after the first. The next four entries are widely separated from each other: in bars 53–54 alto and tenor; in bar 60[1] the tenor with the soprano which enters a half-bar early. Tenor and alto are first combined in bars 85–86, soprano and tenor in bars 93–94. This fugue is full of beauty and euphony, but it cannot be classed, as Riemann suggests, 'among the greatest numbers of the entire work.' For such distinction it is formally not strict enough, but its worth is not reduced because it does not find a place among the most important works in *The Well-Tempered Clavier*.

Performance: quietly flowing, singing. Half note equals 63.

BOOK II: NO. 24 IN B MINOR, BWV 893

The Prelude

(Autograph)

(Altnikol)

If at the end of this second collection of twenty-four preludes and fugues and therefore of both parts of *The Well-Tempered*

[1] Keller: 59. – Tr.

Clavier, we expect a peak or at least an emphatic close, the Prelude and Fugue in B Minor must disappoint us. Quite another end was provided for the first part of *The Well-Tempered Clavier*, the third part of the *Clavierübung* (with the five-voiced Organ Fugue in E Flat Major, BWV 689), and the four parts of the *Clavierübung* (with the Goldberg Variations, BWV 988). Perhaps (although we have no evidence) No. 22 (in B flat minor) was originally in B minor and would have created a splendid closing of the entire work; could it have been transposed down a semitone because there was no B flat minor piece available, leaving the pair of movements making up No. 24 as last-minute substitutes? This can only be conjecture. As Gray remarked, both these B minor pieces could stand equally well elsewhere in Books I or II or in another key, the prelude as a two-part invention, the fugue as a loosely constructed *fughetta*. And yet the prelude has characteristics which indicate the late style of Bach. There are two extant versions distinguished by their time signatures. The first version is, in the autograph, marked *allegro*; the second, is in Altnikol's copy. In the later version, Bach thus telescoped two bars into one, thereby strengthening the formal cohesion of the subject, in which there is no longer a dividing barline. In this way he reverses what he did in the first fugue, when he changed the original c bar into two of 2/4 time. Two more examples of subsequent changing of meter can be found, first in the A Major Fugue for Organ (BWV 536) which, originally in 3/8 time, became lighter and more intimate, as a result of its change to 3/4 time, and second, in the Art of Fugue (BWV 1080) the '*Canon per augmentationem*' which was originally written with the half note as the unit. The change in this movement from *The Well-Tempered Clavier* is the opposite direction to those just mentioned, and there can be no doubt that it is the work of Bach himself. It shows again the aesthetic importance he attached to the choice of meter (in numbering the bars, we follow the second version).

In its motivic elaboration this prelude is an invention; its form is that of a concerto movement whose chief subject describes a circle through the related keys: B minor to D Major (bar 9) to E minor (bar 13) to F sharp minor (bar 21) to B minor (bar 30). The passionate breaking-off of the last exposition in bars 31 and 32 is a sign of his late style (compare the close of the organ chorale '*Vater unser im Himmelreich*,' for manuals only, in the third part of the *Clavierübung*, BWV 682). The connecting episodes (bars 5–6) have a striking similarity to those of the A Minor Prelude in Book II. Its structure is very regular; only in bar 29, where the fermata occurs, are the four-bar groups extended by one bar. The original staccato signs in bars 11, 30 and 32 indicate that the *Affekt* of the prelude should be violent. Quarter note equals 69 (or in the first version half note equals 69).

The Fugue à 3

What should we expect from this last of the 48 fugues with which Bach concludes his work? If not a crown, then indeed a worthy close – but this rather playful little fugue does not provide it. Like the F Major Fugue in Book I, it is a *passepied* in the manner of a fugue. It softens the asperity of the prelude to a comfortable cheerfulness and is thematically connected with it to the extent that the beginning of the subject of the fugue, like that of the prelude, encompasses the chord of B minor; the brisk octave leaps with which it continues are likewise anticipated in the leaps in bars 11 and 12 of the prelude. The subject, with its structure of 2 + 4 bars, begins according to Riemann only with the third and fourth bars (if this is accepted, the elision is almost as charming as that at the beginning of the Overture to *The Marriage of Figaro* by Mozart). The working out throughout lacks the true fugal spirit. Although six entries of the subject follow the exposition, they do not arrange themselves into two expositions in textbook fashion. The caesuras lie elsewhere. As in the B Major Fugue, the countersubject which accompanied the subject in the exposition is abandoned, the trills disappear, and in their place (bar 29) a new countersubject enters, delicately rocking, which has the effect of a harmonic accompaniment to the subject and strengthens its dance-like character. The next main section begins at bar 69. Here the alto and bass throw the

subject back and forth like a ball; it is the bass which holds
the field. At the end Bach gives the fugue a roguish coda of
four bars, whose conception Busoni has deciphered:

Also in this fugue reminiscences of other works appear: the
sequence in bars 87–90 stems from the first episode of the B
Minor Fugue in Book I (bars 17–20), the interweaving of
soprano and alto in bars 50–54 and 92–95 from the G Minor
Fantasy for Organ (BWV 542).

Thus Bach concludes his *Well-Tempered Clavier* almost
lackadaisically, playfully; and yet this last fugue is not un-
important. Like the fugues in F Minor and F Sharp Major in
Book II of *The Well-Tempered Clavier*, it points to the future.
If the venerable form and technique of the fugue were not to
atrophy and dry up, new life had to be brought to it from
outside. In the fugues in F Sharp Major and B Minor, that
new life came from the world of dance. Both point a way
into the future; but the future has not taken advantage of it.
This last fugue has a superbly worked three-voiced structure;
it is distinguished by a playful mastery of fugal technique –
and it is at the same time already a forerunner of the *Davids-
bündler Dances* of Schumann!

Performance: with comfortable grace. Dotted quarter note
equals 56 to 60.

SUPPLEMENT

THE EDITIONS OF 'THE WELL-TEMPERED CLAVIER'

It is beyond the scope of this survey to give even an approximately complete index of the editions of *The Well-Tempered Clavier*. They differ widely in their objectives, and for this reason an attempt has been made to list them according to their faithfulness to the original and to describe them briefly.

A. Facsimile Edition

We are closest to Bach when we study the traits of his own handwriting, and immerse ourselves in their lines. For this, we turn to the published facsimile edition of Book I, which appeared in 1962 with the *Deutsche Verlag für Musik*, Leipzig, edited by Hans Pischner and Karl-Heinz Köhler.

B. 'Urtext' Editions

As far as accuracy is concerned, the totally unedited *Urtext* Edition is next after the facsimile in importance. For those who lack the necessary knowledge and experience of style to use such an *Urtext*, this present volume whose end we have reached may serve as companion and advisor.

The first printings about 1800 were naturally unedited. Decades went by until a critical edition of *The Well-Tempered Clavier* appeared: Franz Kroll published *The Well-Tempered Clavier* in 1862 in the Peters Edition and in 1865 in *Jahrgang XIV* of the edition of the Bach Gesellschaft (with *Revisionsbericht*). Of newer *Urtext* editions should be noted: D. Tovey (Royal School of Music, London) with an introductory essay to every prelude and every fugue within the musical text; Otto von Irmer (G. Henle Verlag, München–Duisburg); Alfred Kreutz published the first part of *The Well-Tempered Clavier* in 1961 in the Peters Edition with separate *Revisionsbericht* and suggestions for performance, Hermann Keller in 1962 the second part, with *Revisionsbericht* as an appendix to the musical text. These editions should supplant the Kroll Edition of 1862.

In the framework of the *New Bach Ausgabe* Walter Gerstenberg will edit *The Well-Tempered Clavier*. The date of its appearance has not yet (1965) been fixed.

The edition of Hans Bischoff with *Steingräber Verlag* (1881) occupies a special position. It is today unfortunately no longer available.[1] Bischoff prepared the musical text on the basis of his own study of the sources, provided variants in the footnotes, and indicated the performance with sparing additions in small print, or enclosed in brackets.

C. *'Edited' Editions*

The first 'edited' edition, and the one which set the editorial standards of *The Well-Tempered Clavier* for many decades, was published by Carl Czerny in 1837. Tempo, dynamics, phrasing, articulation, additional performance signs, precise fingering – all that yielded complete instruction for study and performance. As a student of Beethoven, and conditioned by the outlook of his time, Czerny projected the music of Bach into his own period. Today we reject his often too fast tempi, his continuously changing dynamics, his articulation signs, in short, his often unstylish stylistically incorrect conception. But when his edition appeared, it was an event of great significance, making it possible for thousands of laymen to play Bach; and almost all of the instructive editions in the nineteenth century are more or less dependent on Czerny. Of more recent editions, independent of Czerny mention should be made of those by Albert Schmid-Lindner and Max Reger (*Verlag Schott*).

D. *Interpretive Editions*

In this category must be included an edition for students in which a very important musician and pianist, here Ferruccio Busoni, shares his conception with the reader. Busoni's edition appeared between 1898 and 1915 with Breitkopf und Härtel,

---

[1] In the United States, it is available in the Kalmus reprint. – Tr.

and along with this volume and an *Urtext* edition it can today still be usefully consulted.

THE LITERATURE

From the surprisingly vast literature on Bach, on his clavier works in general and *The Well-Tempered Clavier* in particular, those writings which have served the author particularly in this work are chosen and listed. In certain cases personal remarks have been added:

Friedrich Blume: *Bach im Wandel der Geschichte*, Kassel 1947.

Siegfried Borris: *Die Bearbeitungsverfahren bei den 11 Präludien im Friedemann-Bach-Buch*, in: *Die Musikforschung* 1952, p. 50. (Borris assumes that the versions in the *Klavierbüchlein* are simplifications for Friedemann, those of *The Well-Tempered Clavier*, the originals.)

Hans Brandt-Buys: *Het Wohlt. Klavier*, Arnheim 1942. (The most comprehensive and careful monograph on *The Well-Tempered Clavier*, which has appeared unfortunately only in Dutch.)

Carl von Bruyck: *Analyse des Wohltemperierten Klaviers*, Leipzig 1867. (The first monograph on *The Well-Tempered Clavier*.)

Richard Buchmayer: *Cembalo oder Pianoforte?*, in *Bach-Jahrbuch* 1908, p. 64.

Ludwig Czaczkes: *Analyse des Wohltemperierten Klaviers, Form und Aufbau der Fuge bei Bach*, Volume I, Vienna 1956, Volume 2, 1965. (A penetratrating, strictly scholastic, purely formal analysis of the fugues of *The Well-Tempered Clavier.*)

Carl Dahlhaus: *Bemerkungen zu einigen Fugen des Wohltemperierten Klaviers*, in: *Bach-Jahrbuch* 1954, p. 40.

Versuch über Bachs Harmonik, in: *Bach-Jahrbuch* 1956, p. 73.

Johann Nepomuk David: *Das Wohltemperierte Klavier, Versuch einer Synopsis*, Göttingen 1962, see pp. 23 ff.

S. W. Dehn: *Analyse dreier Fugen aus dem Wohltemperierten Klavier*, Leipzig 1858.

Johann Nikolaus Forkel: *Über Johann Sebastian Bachs Leben, Kunst und Kunstgewerbe*, Leipzig 1802.

J. A. Fuller-Maitland: *J. S. Bach: The "48" (The Well-Tempered Clavier)*, London 1925.

Walter Georgii: *Klaviermusik. Geschichte der Musik für Klavier zu 2 Händen von den Anfängen bis zur Gegenwart*, Berlin/Zurich 2/1950, pp. 121–128.

Walter Gerstenberg: *Zur Verbindung von Präludium und Fuge bei Bach*, Kongressbericht Lüneburg 1950, Kassel 1952, p. 126.

Die Zeitmasse und ihre Ordnungen in Bachs Musik, Lecture in the Bach Festival Week, Ansbach 1951.

Cecil Gray: *The 48 Preludes and Fugues of Bach*, Oxford 1938.

August Halm: *Von zwei Kulturen der Musik*, München 1913. (Contains on page 207 an analysis of the Fugue No. 22 from Book II.)

Hermann Keller: *Die Klavierwerke Bachs*, Leipzig 1950.

Das Tempo bei Bach, in: *Neue Musikzeitschrift* 1950, p. 124.

Die Sequenz bei Bach, in: *Bach-Jahrbuch* 1939, p. 33.

Studien zur Harmonik Bachs, in: *Bach-Jahrbuch* 1934, p. 50.

Die musikalische Artikulation, Kassel 1925.

Phrasierung und Artikulation, Kassel 1953.

Iwan Knorr: *Die Fugen des Wohltemperierten Klaviers in bildlicher Darstellung*, Leipzig 2/1926.

Ernst Kurth: *Die Grundlagen des linearen Kontrapunkts*, Bern 1917.

Wanda Landowska: *Über die C-dur-Fuge des Wohltemperierten Klaviers I*, in: *Bach-Jahrbuch* 1913, p. 53.

Bach und die französische Klaviermusik, in: *Bach-Jahrbuch* 1910.

Ludwig Misch: *Zwei Fugen aus dem Wohltemperierten Klavier in neuer Beleuchtung*, in: *Die Musikforschung* 1952, p. 179.

Unerkannte Formen im Wohltemperierten Klavier, in: *Die Musikforschung* 1948, p. 39.

Ludwig Nissen: *Der Sinn des Wohltemperierten Klaviers II*, in: *Bach-Jahrbuch* 1951/52, p. 54. (A completely abstruse theological interpretation of the Second Book of *The Well-Tempered Clavier!*)

Reinhard Oppel: *Über J. K. F. Fischers Einfluss auf J. S. Bach*, in: *Bach-Jahrbuch* 1910, p. 63.

Zur Fugentechnik Bachs, in: *Bach-Jahrbuch* 1921, p. 9.

Luigi Perrachio: *Il Clavicembalo ben temperato*, Torino 1947.

Paul A. Pisk: *The fugue themes in Bach's Wohltemperierten Klavier*, in: Bulletin of the American Musicological Society 1945.

Erwin Ratz: *Über die Architektonik in den Fugen Bachs*, in: *Österreichische Musikzeitschrift*, 5. Jahrgang.

Musikalische Formenlehre, Vienna 1951.

Albert Schweitzer: *J. S. Bach*, Leipzig 6/1928, especially pp. 295–355.

Marc-André Souchay: *Das Thema in der Fuge Bachs*, in: *Bach-Jahrbuch* 1927 and 1930, p. 1.

Philipp Spitta: *J. S. Bach*, Leipzig 1873 and 1880, especially Volume I, pp. 769 to 784, and Volume II, pp. 663 to 674.

Wilhelm Stade: *Partitur-Analysen der Fugen des Wohltemperierten Klaviers*, Leipzig, without date.

Rudolf Steglich: *J. S. Bach*, Potsdam 1935.

Wege zu Bach, Regensburg 1949.

Das c-moll-Präludium des Wohltemperierten Klaviers I, in: *Bach-Jahrbuch* 1923, p. 1.

Ernst Toch: *Unklarheiten im Schriftbild der cis-moll-Fuge I*, in: *Bach-Jahrbuch* 1923, p. 22.

Wissenschaftliche Bachtagung, Leipzig 1950, Bericht 1951.

Rudolf Wustmann: *Tonartensymbolik zu Bachs Zeit*, in: *Bach-Jahrbuch* 1911, p. 60.

A CLOSING WORD

How did this work (*The Well-Tempered Clavier*), whose completion stretched over more than twenty years, affect its contemporary world and its successors? Little or not at all. The genus of prelude and fugue had lost its significance in the second half of the century. Only in the circle of organists was it still practiced – an organist from Thüringen, Bernhard Christian Weber, wrote a *Wohltemperiertes Klavier* for organ – but the organ too in those decades had lost all importance. Only lesser masters and theoreticians like Marpurg, Kirnberger, Albrechtsberger and others still wrote fugues. For that reason when Bach was resurrected in the nineteenth century, as had happened to very few great artists, he was the old master, the ruler in the realm of counterpoint, on whom generations of composers modeled themselves. For pianists too his works were, above all, splendid exercises in the polyphonic style, taking their place in the approved method of piano study: 'Scales, *études*, Bach, pieces.' Even today *The Well-Tempered Clavier* is more studied than played. It has its secure place in the curriculum and examinations of our music schools and conservatories; preludes and fugues from *The Well-Tempered Clavier* are required in international competitions as test-pieces; they are however just test-pieces. Neither in public concerts, nor on radio, nor in house music does *The Well-Tempered Clavier* play the role for which it was intended. Our highly intellectualized time is more interested in the more abstruse contrapuntal works of Bach – The Musical Offering, the third part of the *Clavierübung*, the Art of the Fugue – than in the middle-of-the-road works, among which *The Well-Tempered Clavier* lies spread out like a great garden. The belief that one should restrict performance of Bach to the harpsichord or clavichord may also be a contributory factor to its neglect in public, although attempts in this direction have not always been encouraging. We are too encumbered theoretically and historically to be able to enjoy *The Well-Tempered Clavier* without prejudice. Here, too, one could speak of the loss of the middle road, if this cliché has not lost its meaning. We must again take possession of this blessed middle road, in which *The Well-Tempered Clavier* finds a place – a position in which depth of thought and joy in playing are equal partners in a harmonious whole. When Bach composed he was neither the fifth evangelist nor a church musician nor a professional *Kapellmeister*, neither a Gothic nor a numerologist – probably something of all of them – but above all he was a musician, so blessed in the 'holy play of art' that he was able to capture in tones the harmony of the world and radiate back to us a transfigured image of ourselves. The play of the twice 24 preludes and fugues is so rich and inexhaustible that we can spend all our lives with it without fathoming its depth.